THE EMPOWERED EXPAT WOMAN

YOUR A-Z GUIDE TO THRIVING WHEREVER YOU ARE

CAMILLA QUINTANA

Copyright © 2024 by Camilla Quintana

All rights reserved. No part of this publication may be reproduced, distributed, or transmitted in any form or by any means, including photocopying, recording, or other electronic or mechanical methods, without the prior written permission of the publisher, except in the case of brief quotations embodied in critical reviews and certain other noncommercial uses permitted by copyright law.

Book Design by HMDPUBLISHING

*I dedicate this book to my sons,
who inspire and motivate me to be a better person and
make our world a better place.*

CONTENTS

PROLOGUE 6
THE EMPOWERED EXPAT WOMEN'S MANIFESTO . . 9
A NEW BEGINNING 11
BECOME YOUR OWN BIGGEST ALLY 15
CLARIFY YOUR GOALS 19
DATING, LOVE & MARRIAGE ACROSS BORDERS 24
EXPAT FATIGUE 29
FINDING YOUR INNER HAPPY PLACE. 33
GIFTS OF EXPAT LIFE. 38
HELPING HANDS 43
IDENTITY CRISIS 47
KEYS TO CROSS-CULTURAL CONFIDENCE 50
JUGGLING LIFE BETWEEN DIFFERENT CULTURES 55
LONELINESS. 58
MAKING A HOME AWAY FROM HOME 63
NETWORKING AND SOCIALIZING ABROAD 66
OWNING WHO YOU ARE 70
POWER OF WORDS 74
QUEEN ENERGY. 77
ROCK BOTTOM ABROAD (AND HOW TO RISE FROM IT). 81
SELF-CARE STRATEGIES FOR EXHAUSTING TIMES ABROAD. 86
THIRD CULTURE KIDS 93
UNCERTAINTY 97

VISION	100
WINNING MINDSETS	105
XXX YOUR LIFE ABROAD	112
YEARNING FOR HOME	117
ZEST FOR GLOBAL LIVING	121
FINAL WORDS	125

PROLOGUE

To the courageous women navigating life abroad, this book is for you.

Whether you're enjoying the good times, struggling with the bad ones, or embracing the messy beauty in between, you're in the right place. This isn't just a book; it's a celebration of your journey, a testament to your resilience, and an invitation to embrace your Empowered Expat Woman within!

For The Unapologetically Real

Life abroad consists of highs, lows, ups and downs. Your journey is unique, and every feeling and sensation you experience is valid. Let's ditch the glossy facade, break down the stereotypes and dive into the real, nuanced experiences of cross-border life.

For The Misinterpreted

No more sidelining the expat woman as a secondary character, dismissing her concerns as trivial, or presuming she's on an endless vacation. This book takes a clear stance: our perspectives as accompanying partners, expat entrepreneurs and professionals, digital nomads, mothers of Third Culture Kids, and any other role we may identify with are diverse and important. It's time to bring these perspectives into the spotlight.

For The Courageous

In our results-driven world, trying one's best, over and over again, is so underrated. I happen to believe that the commitment to try your best, the willingness to see the glass half full, and the leap of faith to trust in your path ahead are some of the most honorable traits you can possess! Here's to you, who never gives up hope, who courageously stands up again after falling, and keeps moving forward.

For Those Ready To Embrace Their Power

Let's engage in honest conversations that connect and empower. It's about reclaiming and rewriting our narrative, and standing as our own biggest allies.

A Culmination of Experience

All of the ideas and insights presented in this book aren't just theories; they were inspired by the countless lived experiences, both of myself and of my clients. Reflecting on two decades of expat living and years of coaching fellow expats has served as a wellspring of inspiration. I've poured so much passion and dedication into creating profound and original content for 'The Empowered Expat Woman' podcast, my blog, and keynote speeches. This book consolidates and assembles the insights and wisdom gathered over the years.

How To Use This Book

Think of this book as your coach, companion and confidant, guiding you every step of the way in your expat journey. The best thing about it? There's no need to follow a straight line. You can easily jump back and forth between chapters, picking the ones that best match your current situation.

So whether you're delving into the ABCs or flipping to the XYZs, each chapter stands on its own, ready to offer valuable insights. Just as the book's title suggests, its structure is designed to empower you to navigate your own adventure!

Bonus Material

To get the most out of this book and dive even deeper into the insights you'll get, head to www.camillaquintana.com/book now and access your free extras and bonus material!

May you find strength, inspiration, and support within these pages. And remember, you're never alone. We're all figuring out this expat life together!

THE EMPOWERED EXPAT WOMEN'S MANIFESTO

Empowered Expat Women are the new changemakers:
Trailblazers, finding new paths and crossing frontiers.
Connectors, bringing the world closer together.

A global lifestyle is the new unfair advantage:
Wherever we go we leave a piece of ourselves,
yet we become fuller, richer and more complete.

With our multifaceted backgrounds and experiences,
We color the world in new shades of hope.

We re-define identity and re-imagine belonging
because we know our place in the world
is waiting for us to be claimed.

Empathy is our superpower.
We see through to the core of people,
hidden underneath layers of cultural conditioning.

Authenticity intrigues us.
As we learn to embrace our distinctiveness,
we enable others to do the same.

In a world where borders separate,
We can find commonalities and build bridges.

Because we know we're stronger together,
We create sisterhoods that become family.

We ask for help, support and a shoulder to cry on.
And once we've replenished, we return the favor.

We love connection but don't fear solitude.
We are seeking allies, but deep down we know
that we're our own biggest one.

Empowered Expat Women are the new visionaries.
We choose to see opportunities where others encounter obstacles.

We're committed to finding our portable sense of purpose
and learning to creatively adapt it to our changing circumstances.

We are the authors of our life story. One we'll love to tell....
In a foreign language. To our new expat bestie. To our grandchildren.

Now it's our time to soar.
Call us Empowered Expat Women, and watch us roar.

A New Beginning

Whether it starts with a relocation, a new year, month, or week, or simply by opening this book: there's something incredibly powerful about a new beginning! It's an invitation to reflect on the past, let go of what no longer serves you, and, most importantly, think about what you want from life. A new chapter abroad offers a chance to envision and reimagine what you want your relationships, career, and every aspect of your life to look like - and then go after it!

If you're about to or have recently relocated, chances are you're filled with excitement and have a long list of things to do. Settling into and exploring a new host country can keep you very busy and distracted - I know! This phase is often referred to as the 'Honeymoon Phase' of living abroad, and by all means, enjoy it!

But also, take a moment to think about how you can best leverage the momentum that comes with this new beginning, so that you can set yourself up for success and make the most of your time abroad in the longer run.

Momentum is an incredibly powerful force that drives us towards greater well-being, success, and fulfillment. There's just one catch: once it fades, it becomes increasingly difficult to make changes in our lives. Ever heard of Newton's first law of motion? It basically says that things like to keep doing what they're doing, whether that's resting or being in motion.

So, starting something new becomes much easier when you're already riding the natural flow of momentum. Once that slows down, however, you'll need to bring up a good dose of energy – the mental and emotional kind – to get moving again.

An additional factor is that, once we settle into our status quo and grow accustomed to it, we tend to stop noticing areas of improvement. It's just like with that lamp I didn't buy for our dining room after our last move. At first, I spent time browsing catalogs and window shopping. But as days turned into weeks and the momentum of our move shifted to a daily routine, I became so used to that lonesome light bulb hanging from the ceiling that I stopped noticing it. It's a scenario we often find ourselves in: when we become used to less-than-ideal situations, we can lose sight of what's wrong with them and fail to take action. Dangerous territory!

Now, that lamp was just an object, but when it comes to your life, you certainly wouldn't want to settle for less, right? Unfolding your full potential and creating a fulfilling life should be your top priority, and momentum plays a significant role in achieving this. The key to prolonging this phase for as long as possible is to set meaningful and specific goals that excite you, and then commit to working towards them. Sure, living in the moment and going with the flow has its merits. But having personal goals that truly inspire you and give your life purpose is even better.

This is especially important for Expat Women like you and me. We need to navigate new and changing surroundings, cultures, and circumstances; we find ourselves starting over from scratch, possibly several times, and often lack a sense of certainty, continuity, or a support system to catch us when we fall. I've worked with many Expat Women who, once they had settled in, struggled to find fulfilling ways to spend their days. Whether it's because of work restrictions, loneliness, or limited opportunities, feeling constantly unchallenged and uninspired is painful. It made me realize how crucial it is for us to feel like our daily activities matter and have meaning. We need to feel valued, capable and like we're making a difference.

That's why I encourage you to take the time to figure out what truly matters to you, formulate clear goals, and hold yourself accountable to reach them. This will not only give your life more meaning, purpose, and direction but also make you feel safe and significant.

As you're working towards fulfilling your inspiring goals, do:

- Celebrate your efforts and progress along the way!

- Adopt a 'growth mindset': it's not about getting perfect results quickly, but about believing in your ability to continuously learn, improve, and progress through hard work, effort, and resilience.

- Surround yourself with supportive and inspiring people, that add extra fuel to the fire and keep your momentum going strong.

Here are three questions to ask yourself that will help you embark on this new chapter:

- What would it take to make my experience in my host country truly great and worthwhile?

- What do I expect to gain from living abroad?

- What's one big and bold action step I could take to achieve this?

If you can harness the momentum of this new beginning, there will be no stopping you from pursuing a truly inspiring and meaningful life plan!

Want to have a closer look into which areas of your life are thriving and which others will need your attention in order to get back into balance? Then take the "Wheel of Expat Life Quiz" - which you can access free of charge at www.camillaquintana.com/book

Become Your Own Biggest Ally

If I had to choose the one thing that's made the biggest difference in my own expat life, it would be this: becoming my own biggest ally. People, things, and experiences come and go, but the one constant presence you can always rely on is yourself.

As global women, it sometimes feels like we don't have anyone in our corner (or at least, we never seem to have 'home advantage'). We face ups and downs, navigate changes and uncertainties, and often lack a support system to lean on. That's why it's crucial to become your own safe haven - the place you can turn to when the storm hits and life gets tough.

I've always been an advocate for practicing radical self-love and nurturing the relationship we have with ourselves. While other relationships may seem more important, it's the way we relate to ourselves that truly shapes the quality of our connections with others. It also influences the actions we take, the choices we make, and how we live our lives.

No matter where you go, you always carry yourself with you. So let's make sure you're not just lugging around extra baggage, but rather, that you're carrying your ever-supportive self as your ultimate ally!

An ally is someone who is always on your side, supporting you, sharing your vision and values, and whom you can trust to do what's in your best interest. An ally is not scared to go through discomfort if it's for the sake of a meaningful long-term goal. That's why I prefer this analogy over the famous one of 'being your own best friend'. A friend might be more focused on what's good for you in the short term, or even have their own agenda.

There are many ways to cultivate this allyship. But I've found that the most powerful starting point is developing a constructive, compassionate, and respectful inner dialogue. You see, our inner voices play a significant role in shaping our self-perception and influencing our actions. The way you speak to yourself directly impacts your self-esteem, self-confidence, and overall well-being.

When you have encouraging and supportive self-talk, it uplifts your spirits, motivates you to give things a try, and helps you bounce back from setbacks. On the other hand, negative self-talk can erode your self-belief, create self-doubt, and thus limit your potential. By consciously managing your inner voices and cultivating a positive and empowering self-talk, you're not only nurturing a strong alliance with yourself, but also setting the foundation for personal growth, resilience and success in life.

This has a lot to do with developing self-leadership skills. Personally, I like to think of myself as the CEO of my mind and body. It helps me create some distance from those inner voices that like to chatter away, and realize that they don't define me. I am the one who hears and observes them. As their CEO, I'm in a capacity to decide which voices I listen to and take into account.

To manage your inner voices, start by identifying them and getting to know their characteristics. Do you have a vocal

Inner Critic, a voice that puts you down and blames you? Or perhaps an *Inner Worrier,* always anxious about potential problems on the horizon? Maybe there's an *Inner Complainer* running wild, constantly pointing out what's wrong. Take some time to become aware of those voices, give them a name and understand them.

Remember, just like people in real life, our inner voices aren't all good or all bad. They try to help or protect us in their own way. For example, your Inner Critic may push you to work harder and anticipate mistakes, while your Inner Worrier might prompt you to create backup plans for security. Your Inner Complainer might actually highlight when something doesn't align with your values or isn't good for you, helping you to set better boundaries.

However, it's important to keep these voices in check. When they start taking over and consuming your thoughts, they do more harm than good. They hold you back, make you feel insecure, unworthy, or depressed. And that's <u>not</u> what an ally does!

Let's try the following: Think of your inner voices as your advisory board, and of yourself as the CEO in charge. Instead of trying to silence them completely (which will hardly be possible anyway), consider reassigning their roles, training them, or reducing the time they get to speak up. Also, think about which voices are missing on your team. Could there be a need for more self-compassion or optimism to balance things out?

The analogy of the advisory board helps to raise your awareness of your inner dialogue and empowers you to manage it for your own benefit. When you realize that you're not those voices, but their leader, you gain the ability to create new ways of thinking and integrate different parts of yourself. Developing a constructive, compassionate, and respectful inner dialogue is a huge step toward becoming your own biggest ally!

As you continue reading this book, you'll find various other concepts that will help you to strengthen and solidify your inner allyship even more.

On our expat journeys we sometimes forget,
That we are our own greatest asset,

To be our own ally, activate internal forces
Instead of seeking approval from external sources

We'll believe in our dreams and our aspirations,
And fuel ourselves with our own motivations.

We'll learn to trust our instincts and intuition,
Relentlessly working towards our own long term vision,

No matter what, we've got our own back
So we'll focus on abundance, not on what we lack

There will be times we'll feel lost or alone,
And like there is no place we can call our 'home',

That's our cue to turn inward, tap into our strength
And become our own support system, at any length

To be our own lighthouse, that beacon of light,
Guiding us home, to our happy place inside

It's time to become our own power plug,
To recharge and replenish through radical self-love

Become your own biggest ally, starting today
And you'll thrive wherever you are, in every way

Clarify Your Goals

Living an international lifestyle is adventurous, full of unexpected turns and gains. It's a path that's certainly not set in stone, and quite possibly, the desire to avoid living a mundane, planned-out life was one of the reasons that made you move abroad in the first place.

But this freedom to shape your life comes with its own set of challenges, leading to moments of uncertainty and sleepless nights. Trust me, I've been there too. Feeling overwhelmed by choices, stuck in indecision, unsure of where to turn next – these are common experiences for many Expat Women on their international journeys. Questions start to swirl: Where should I live? How long should I stay? What path should I take for myself and my family?

When standing at such a crossroads, you might start to overthink, ruminate, and go around in circles. It becomes difficult to see the light at the end of the tunnel when you don't even know which direction to look. Through my years of working with Expat Women, I've discovered that the real underlying problem in these situations is often a lack of clarity of three crucial aspects:

1. You don't know what your long-term vision is (for yourself and your family)

2. You're unsure of your most important values, needs, and motivators

3. You don't have a plan for how to further tap into your potential, internal resources, and opportunities

Understanding the importance of clarity is like finding the key to a treasure chest. I like to say: "Clarity leads to confidence, and confidence leads to inspired action." When you have crystal-clear answers to the above points, taking the right steps forward becomes second nature.

If you're wondering what might be getting in the way of your clarity, don't worry. It's quite common and can be caused by various factors. Firstly, the demands of our daily lives can be overwhelming. Between work, family responsibilities, household chores, and constant phone notifications, it's easy to prioritize the seemingly urgent matters over the most important and fulfilling tasks in the long run. Another common factor is that many foreigners, as well as moms and caregivers, often find themselves overly aware of and focused on meeting others' expectations, leading to a conflict between their personal aspirations and societal pressures. When you add the challenges of navigating life in a different language and culture, it's no wonder that clarity about our deepest desires takes a backseat

So what can you do about this? Let's apply a simple, yet profound principle:

ALWAYS START WITH THE END IN MIND

If you're feeling stuck or uncertain, it's likely because you've lost sight of or are unclear of your long-term vision. When your life is infused with meaning and purpose, everything falls into place like pieces of a puzzle, creating a unique big picture. Each experience, each challenge, becomes a chapter in your very own book of life. With a clear vision as your guiding star, you'll navigate obstacles with ease and make better decisions - the ones that align with your aspirations.

THE ART OF GOAL GETTING

Now that we've uncovered the magic of having a clear vision for your international life, let's talk strategy.

As a Coach, I know how important it is to help my clients formulate clear goals, break them down into action steps, as well as to encourage and hold them accountable. Here are four strategies I like to employ, tailored to suit different personalities and circumstances:

Daily Baby-Steps:

Inspired by James Clear's book *Atomic Habits*, this approach focuses on making small, consistent changes over time. By aiming for just a 1% improvement each day, you can see remarkable progress over the course of a year. Making very small changes over time might not sound or feel very exciting at first. But don't be fooled: you're building a habit that will stay with you, plus, you'll reap the benefits of the compound effect (= Choices + Behavior + Habits + Time).

This approach will work for anyone, but if you're someone who's got a lot on your plate and already feels overwhelmed as it is, this might be your go-to strategy.

The Heart Project:

This approach is more intuitive, allowing you to pursue a big goal with excitement and passion. When you're deeply inspired by an idea, you'll naturally find ways to progress towards it without needing a strict framework. It's about entering a state of flow, where you're deeply engaged, productive and wholeheartedly dedicated to the project. Your heart project is usually carried out within a specific timeframe, with a clear beginning and end. Due to its immersive and creative nature, it's best not to drag it out for too long, as you might burn yourself out.

The 3-Year Plan:

This concept has been a game-changer for many Expat Women I've had the privilege to work with. In today's fast-paced world, there's often an urgency to accomplish everything immediately, but this mindset can lead to burnout and rob us of the joy of the journey.

I say New Year's Resolutions are overrated. Instead, consider the luxury, freedom, and inspiration of crafting a 3-year plan for yourself. This approach leaves room and flexibility for pregnancies, relocations, or other life events, which is particularly relevant for Expat Women. On the other hand, it encourages you to think bigger, allowing you to set more ambitious and meaningful goals for yourself over a longer period of time.

Setting Weekly / Monthly Goals:

Ideal for those who thrive on structure and organization, this strategy involves breaking down larger objectives into smaller, achievable tasks on a weekly or monthly basis. By setting clear priorities and deadlines, you can maintain momentum and track their progress effectively. Whether it's outlining specific actions for each day or broader objectives for the month, this approach ensures accountability and can be a great roadmap for success.

SURROUND YOURSELF WITH THE RIGHT PEOPLE

Lastly, it's important to leverage the positive influence other people can have on us. Sharing your goals with someone you trust and who will cheer you on makes the journey a whole lot more fun and keeps you accountable. Be conscious about building a network of people who share and understand your goals. This way, you can support and inspire each other.

On the other hand, try to keep away from people who are critical, judgmental, and jealous. Sometimes, seeing you do well can make them feel bad about themselves. These people, often called 'energy vampires,' might try to bring you down so it's best to stay away from their negativity. You deserve to be around people who truly want to see you do well and shine!

Now that you've clarified your goals and set yourself up for success, let's not forget that it's not just about reaching the final destination. Celebrate the little wins along the way, because each step you take brings you closer to living a fulfilled life!

Download your fillable goal-getter template at www.camillaquintana.com/book

Dating, Love & Marriage Across Borders

Falling in love with someone from a different culture is exhilarating! Multi-colored butterflies; that 'Us against the world' feeling; or finding that gratifying affirmation that love can indeed conquer borders.

To me, one of the most exciting aspects is that you're able to dive into a different world through your significant other. And not only that, you also get to experience being *you* in a different cultural context, speaking a different language and adopting new customs...

In a world where long-term relationships and marriage are often labeled 'boring', our inter-cultural connections seem like a promising alternative to the oh-so-predictable rut.

Having lived in different countries in my youth, befriending and dating people from different cultures has certainly enriched me in many ways. I don't think it came to anyone's surprise when, upon my return to my hometown, Vienna, I started dating a handsome Spaniard, with whom I had previously bonded over life in Madrid, Spanish music and jamón ibérico.

Fast forward a few years, we got married in a beautiful bilingual ceremony and bi-cultural celebration. As I write these lines, we've been happily married for over 10 years, lived in 3 different countries, and welcomed 3 little global citizens into our family.

While the saying 'opposites attract' may have brought you and your partner together, being on the same page will be a determining factor in whether your relationship will endure. Here are a few things you can do to align yourselves and hopefully avoid culturally-related misunderstandings, clashes, and crises!

1. ADDRESS THE DIFFERENCES

We often assume that we know about our partner's culture, background, and views. But the truth is that each human being is very complex, we all go through different phases and are on unique journeys of growth. Therefore, I recommend dedicating a romantic evening or two to playing detective and getting genuinely curious about each other's perspectives, similarities, and differences on certain subjects and values.

You might be surprised by your partner's answers, or maybe you'll even surprise yourself. Remember, there are no right or wrong responses as long as they come from the heart.

Here's a list of topics you could discuss:

- **Communication style:** Do you appreciate directness and bluntness, or do you believe that you catch more flies with honey than vinegar?
- **Punctuality:** Do you consider it vital to arrive on time, or are you flexible to adapt meeting times based on certain conditions?
- **Planning:** Do you try to avoid risk and uncertainty by planning ahead, or do you prefer going with the flow and figuring things out along the way?

- **Promises:** How do you view promises? Are they set in stone, or can circumstances alter them?

- **(Extended) Family:** Who is family to you? What are your obligations towards them? How often would you like to gather, and how much influence should they have on your life?

- **Individualism:** Do you think couples should live life according to their own goals and desires, or should they consider the customs and needs of their community, family, and culture? Where would you draw a line?

- **Husband/Boyfriend:** What does this role mean to each of you? What are some traits and responsibilities you attribute to it?

- **Wife/Girlfriend:** What does this role mean to each of you? What are some traits and responsibilities you attribute to it?

- **Fatherhood:** What are your expectations and role models for being a good dad?

- **Motherhood:** What are your expectations and role models for being a good mom?

- **Home country/culture:** Do you have a home country and culture? Which aspects resonate with you, and which others don't? Would you like to live there one day or raise your children there?

- **Religion:** Are you religious? How important is faith to you? How does it inform your decisions, choices, and customs? How would you like to raise your children?

Download the free resource to make this exercise more fun at www.camillaquintana.com/book

2. CREATE COMMONALITIES

When I got married, one of the best pieces of advice I received was to create new traditions as a new family unit. Every family has its own customs, and every culture has unique traditions. If you and your partner are expats who have lived in different countries, just imagine the beautiful blends you can create with such diverse ingredients!

Make a list of special occasions you treasure and would like to continue, adopt, or expand. This can include religious holidays, New Year's Eve/Day, Valentine's Day, Thanksgiving, Halloween, national holidays, birthdays, and even fun weekly events like 'Taco Tuesdays' or 'Friday's Movie Night.'

Especially if you're planning to start a family or already have children, this exercise will enrich your family life and allow you to create your very own beautifully blended family culture.

3. DON'T USE 'CULTURE' AGAINST YOUR PARTNER

Cultural conditioning is real. Many things that are considered normal in one culture might be unusual in another. This applies not only to obvious aspects, like greetings or gestures, but also to subtle factors, such as how we process and transmit information, what we subconsciously associate with certain terms or how we perceive situations.

During times of stress, these cultural differences can quickly become the center of a hurricane. We might generalize or stereotype, saying things like, 'All of you [insert nationality] are so...' or '[insert country] is just so...!'

While there may be some truth to these statements, using them turns any argument between two people into a fight between two countries, cultures, or religions.

Sometimes it can feel deeply satisfying to let your frustration out on an entire country, especially if you've moved there and feel marginalized in some way. However, stereotyping, generalizing, and simplifying is hurtful and always fails to address issues at their core. It's not fair play, and instead of finding a solution, you might end up creating an even bigger problem.

Another common issue in intercultural couples is subjecting one partner to unfair comparisons. This often happens when the couple lives in one partner's country, and there's a lack of cultural references for the foreign partner. It's tempting to expect them to 'just be like the others' and conform to the way things are done there. But the foreign partner is not a local, and will never fully be. And that's a good thing!

Rather than trying to change them, create space for them to hold onto their own identity, customs, and traditions. Focus on their unique strengths, values, and interests. There's a reason you fell in love and chose your foreign partner, so if the local, mainstream culture makes you forget, make an effort to remember what initially attracted you to them.

Travel and visit your partner's home country often, collect experiences, make friends, and build references. If possible, consider moving there or to a neutral ground for some time. A multicultural relationship should never require sacrificing one's identity, culture, or point of view. Instead, it should celebrate and merge both backgrounds, appreciating the uniqueness of your union.

Look for other intercultural couples or guides and build your own support system to navigate the ups and downs of your relationship. By doing so, you can establish a strong foundation for a fulfilling and harmonious partnership across borders.

E

Expat Fatigue

Have you heard of 'Expat Fatigue'? It's that weary feeling that settles in after living in a place for a considerable amount of time, when the initial excitement has faded, and you find yourself stuck in a rut, lacking perspective and motivation.

Expat Fatigue can arise for various reasons: Maybe your expectations of what life abroad would be like haven't been met. Perhaps you're tired of constantly relocating and yearn for stability and a fixed address. It's possible that conflicts with your significant other or someone close to you are taking a toll on your overall well-being in your host country. Sometimes, the local conditions, culture, climate, people, or cuisine can start to get on your nerves. And of course, longing for home and familiarity can be another significant factor.

If you resonate with any of these scenarios, don't worry. I've worked with many individuals experiencing Expat Fatigue, and I've come up with a 3-step plan that can help you navigate and overcome it.

STEP 1: CHANGE YOUR STATE

Have you ever wondered why people often struggle to make the necessary changes to create a fulfilled life, despite having access to great advice, tools, and hacks? It's because their current state of mind doesn't align with the mindset needed to adopt and implement those changes!

Think about it: when you're in a low state of mind, battling fears, doubts, and insecurities, it's challenging to jump right into confidently and assertively solving the problem. There's simply too big a gap between where your head and feelings currently are and where you want to be. Therefore, changing your state becomes a prerequisite for effectively changing your circumstances.

So, how can you change your state? Here are a few practices you can adopt at any time, regardless of what's happening around and inside you:

- **Practice Self-Compassion**

When you're feeling down, the last thing you need is to feel bad or ashamed about that. Be kind to yourself, especially during tough times. Instead of forcing yourself to feel great again when you genuinely don't, take baby steps. Acknowledge and accept your feelings. It's okay to have an off-day, week, or phase. Give yourself permission to go through these moments without judgment.

Also, get into the habit of regularly checking in with yourself and ask: "What do I need right now? What is one thing I could do, think, or say to myself to feel a little better?" Treating yourself with love and care is vital for improving your state and well-being.

- **Fix your posture**

Have you ever noticed how your body responds when you're feeling down? Your shoulders slump, you find yourself slouching, and your breathing becomes shallow. Your posture communicates to your brain the mental state you're in.

By consciously changing your physical state and posture, you can actually influence your emotional state as well. It's a powerful way to interrupt negative thought patterns and send signals of vitality to your brain, almost as if to reassure yourself, "Hey, it's okay, I'm safe, and I can relax now!"

There are several quick and effective ways to change your physical state. Start by taking deep breaths to ground yourself and soothe your nervous system. Make your exhale slightly longer than your inhale. If you find yourself sitting down for long periods, disrupt that routine by moving your body - jump around, stretch, or take a refreshing walk outside. Dancing to a favorite song (possibly from your youth or a more careless time?), exercising to release feel-good endorphins or even laughing, are all powerful ways to shift your physical state and uplift your mood.

- **Practice Gratitude**

Expressing gratitude can quickly change your state and make you feel brighter. Take a few moments each day to reflect on the things you're grateful for, whether big or small. Gratitude is one of the most powerful, positive feelings, and it's virtually impossible to feel both grateful and miserable at the same time.

STEP 2: THE QUICK FIXES

Quick fixes are like band-aids for wounds: they may not cure what's caused the bleeding but they can still provide temporary relief and protection, so I believe they're valuable tools.

Consider these quick fixes:

- **Add some variety to your life**

    Why not break out of the routine and become a 'tourist on a mission'? Create challenges for yourself, for instance to visit a number of local sights, discover hidden gems and different boroughs, try different restaurants or explore local farmer's markets… What can you do to add some excitement to each day?

- **Make your home feel more like home**

  Your home should be a sanctuary - a place of refuge, calm, and safety. Even small touches like buying fresh flowers, putting up photos of loved ones, or creating a happy place corner can make a significant difference in your overall well-being.

- **Look for company**

  Building connections is crucial, especially when you're living abroad. Regardless of whether you consider yourself an introvert or extrovert, human beings thrive on social interactions. Reach out to people you already know and make an effort to meet new ones. If you find that difficult, explore online communities and seek positive and uplifting interactions there.

STEP 3: CREATE A LONG-TERM VISION

If you're grappling with Expat Fatigue and are feeling unsure about your life and your future abroad, it's probably because you haven't defined or have lost sight of your long-term vision.

Having a clear vision automatically brings more meaning, clarity, and inner drive to your everyday life. It's like the ultimate therapy to combat Expat Fatigue.

In conclusion, Expat Fatigue is a common challenge that many people face when living abroad. By following the 3-step plan of changing your state, implementing quick fixes, and creating an enticing long-term vision, you can overcome this fatigue and let your expat adventure unfold with renewed energy and purpose!

Finding Your Inner Happy Place

A few years ago, my husband and I were preparing for yet another international relocation. He was already traveling back and forth for work, and the kids and I were going to move in the summer.

At the time, we were living in my hometown, Vienna, and honestly, my life was easy, fun, smooth, and full of plans and people. So despite my previous international lifestyle, the thought of moving away and starting over from scratch somewhere else didn't excite me at all.

Nevertheless, I spent these months not only preparing for the move but also preparing my mind for this next chapter. You see, during my first experience of following my spouse abroad for his job a few years prior, I had felt disempowered in many ways. This time around, I made a firm decision: I was going to find a way to make this experience absolutely worthwhile - not just for my family but for me as an individual. And I was going to thrive, no matter what.

I can still vividly remember myself standing in my beautiful kitchen, my 'happy place' filled with countless memories I knew I would miss: cooking with friends, enjoying mealtime with my small children, studying for my first Coach Diploma, and setting up my very first website.

As I reminisced about those happy moments, I expected to feel a wave of emotions, a burst of nostalgia, or maybe shedding a tear or two. But to my surprise, there was nothing. It was as if those memories lived within me, and were completely unattached to my kitchen.

I picked up the phone and called my sister in Australia, who's my trusted confidant. "You know what I realized?" I said to her, "With my international lifestyle, I can't tie my happiness to a specific location. But I have my 'Inner Happy Place'. No one can ever take that away from me, and I will always be at home there."

That realization was incredibly empowering, liberating, and comforting. I coined the term 'Inner Happy Place' to describe that deep and authentic connection with yourself. It's a feeling of intrinsic belonging, safety, wholeness, and being at home within yourself. This concept has brought comfort and solace not only to me but also to my community of women living an international lifestyle.

Rupi Kaur said, "Loneliness is a sign that you're in desperate need for yourself." Today, I truly understand what she means. I used to search for external sources to make me feel complete and connected, whether it was a physical happy place, people or possessions. Your Inner Happy Place is yours forever, and completely portable. It's like an inner embrace, an anchor, a true sense of home.

To discover your Inner Happy Place, it's essential to shift your focus inward and place more energy on yourself rather than external things and people. Learn to sit with yourself through changing emotions, thoughts, and experiences. Make peace with all aspects of yourself - the beautiful, the good, and the not-so-good.

When you can embrace all of you, living within your mind and body becomes an incredibly satisfying, supportive, and secure experience! It grounds you during relocations, offers comfort and companionship during lonely times, and provides a safe haven during periods of uncertainty or stress.

Here are a few practices that will help you cultivate your Inner Happy Place and empower you to live a truly connected life:

- **Self-Awareness:**

    Take the time to truly know and understand yourself. Get into the habit of asking questions like "What do I think about this?", "How do I feel right now?", or "How would I rather feel and what do I need to do to achieve that?". Reflect on your values, passions, strengths, and aspirations - they will guide your decisions and inspire your goals in life. Knowing yourself profoundly gives you a solid foundation to build your Inner Happy Place on.

- **Self-Love and Compassion:**

    Life is so much better when you feel good about being yourself! Make it your number one priority to always treat yourself with kindness, forgiveness, and compassion.

This will significantly impact the way you show up and live your life, and will help you be more present, positive and resourceful. Engage in regular self-care practices that nourish your body, mind, and soul. As you cultivate self-love, you will also find it easier to extend that same compassion to others, fostering meaningful connections and relationships.

- **Mindset Work:**

  We all experience limiting beliefs and negative self-talk that hold us back. However, by becoming aware of them, courageously challenging their validity, and skillfully reframing them, we can liberate ourselves from their power.

  Adopting a growth mindset will also go a long way. With this way of thinking you believe in your ability to improve and learn new things with effort and practice. It's okay to make mistakes, to dust yourself off and to try again when you believe in your potential to become better and achieve your goals in due course.

- **Meditation and Mindfulness:**

  By now, most of us know that integrating meditation into our daily lives has multiple, significant, and scientifically proven benefits on our health. So why do so many people still not take advantage of them?

  If the image of sitting cross-legged in silence on a cushion doesn't appeal to you, don't worry. There are many more options out there for you, and it's important to find the one that suits your preferences and start from there. You can try silent, guided, or physically active meditations, as well as mindfulness exercises, prayer, or gratitude practices. Personally, I really enjoy listening to binaural beats or practicing Yin Yoga. Take your time to explore and discover what works best for you on your journey to find peace and clarity within yourself.

- **An Attitude of Gratitude:**

When we make it a habit to acknowledge and value our blessings and joys, even the small ones we once overlooked, we have the power to completely transform our life experience, perspective and outlook. Set aside dedicated moments each day to immerse yourself in the warmth and beauty of profound gratitude. When fixating on what you lack, thank yourself for the insight. Then, gently redirect your thoughts to what you already have or how your skills can improve the situation.

- **Living a Healthy Lifestyle:**

    Just as you wouldn't neglect your physical surroundings, your Inner Happy Place also requires care and nurturing. Fuel your body with nutritious food that energizes and sustains you. Make conscious choices that prioritize your well-being, such as regular exercise, sufficient sleep, and stress management. By taking care of your physical health, you create a solid foundation for mental and emotional well-being - another prerequisite to tap into your Inner Happy Place.

Your Inner Happy Place thrives on all of the above. I hope you'll adopt these habits, I because there's no greater reward than to be able to feel at home with yourself.

G
Gifts Of Expat Life

Without a doubt, an international lifestyle comes with many wonderful things. As you're reading this, you might be completely sold on the idea of living abroad, or maybe you're currently at a crossroads, questioning whether you've made the right decision and where to go from here...

Either way, this list of 15 benefits and rewards of expat life will reassure you at best, and help you sleep better at night at the very least. Feel free to hang this list somewhere to reassure yourself - or pass it on to those relatives that just don't understand your international lifestyle!

1. **Re-discovering Yourself:**

Being able to redefine and discover who you are, who you want to be, and who you could be, beyond the conscious or subconscious restrictions you may have encountered back home, is priceless. Moving overseas makes you realize that your self-image, beliefs, and values are conditioned and therefore optional. It can be profoundly liberating to consciously think about who you want to be on your own terms. Don't underestimate this privilege!

2. **Broadening Your Horizon and Worldview:**

Living overseas provides the opportunity to immerse yourself in new cultures and learn about different ways of life. You'll gain an international perspective, allowing you to view the world through a broader lens and understand global issues from different angles. This can open many doors for you and make you a much more aware, well-rounded, and understanding human being.

3. **Enhancing Your Language Skills:**

Living in a foreign country is one of the best ways to learn a new language or improve your language skills. Languages have opened so many doors for me, both personally and professionally. They are the gateway to culture, allowing you to comprehend and immerse yourself more deeply in it. Furthermore, learning foreign languages brings numerous proven benefits, from enhanced cognitive function and communication skills to increased academic performance and job opportunities.

4. **Gaining Independence:**

While some foreigners may experience the opposite, make no mistake: finding your way in a new country, culture, and context will make you more independent, self-sufficient, and resourceful in the long run. It can be liberating to live your life miles away from the expectations placed upon you back home and be able to make your own rules. Also, learning to cope with feelings of loneliness and isolation is a valuable life lesson that will make you more self-reliant.

5. **Making New Friends and Building a Global Network:**

Living overseas allows you to meet new people from different backgrounds, which can lead to meaningful, lifelong friendships. Personally, I've learned so much from my international friends, many of whom have significantly contributed to my understanding of friendship and what it means to be a good friend.

Broadening the pool of people you meet increases your chances of bonding with like-minded, interesting, and inspiring individuals from across the globe. In our interconnected world, having a strong global network is a clear asset in your personal and professional life. It provides numerous benefits, such as access to new ideas, opportunities, and perspectives, expanding horizons and granting countless opportunities for growth and success.

6. **Developing Cultural Awareness and Intercultural Competence:**

In today's globalized world, cultural awareness and sensitivity are important skills. Immersing yourself in a new culture allows for a deeper understanding of different perspectives and ways of life. It challenges assumptions and stereotypes, turning you into a potential change-maker and valuable interlocutor. An added benefit? Your cross-cultural experiences will help you relate better to different people and give you great conversation topics.

7. **Building Resilience:**

Resilience is the ability to bounce back from setbacks, challenges, and adversity. Building it is essential because it allows us to better cope with difficult situations. As expats, we definitely have an advantage in this department! Life abroad is full of ups and downs, frustrating paperwork, culture clashes, and other challenges that are a natural part of the journey. By developing resilience, we'll adopt a more positive outlook on life, become more adaptable to change, reduce anxiety and increase our overall well-being.

8. **Developing Professional Skills:**

Living overseas can provide valuable experience for your resume. Not only will you be able to add 'cross-cultural communication and language skills' to your list, but you will also gain new opportunities for professional growth and development, including exposure to new industries and business practices. In fact, many of my clients have started their own businesses or projects abroad, leveraging the rich experiences their global lifestyle has granted them.

9. **Meeting Your Need for Adventure:**

If you've chosen to live abroad, it's likely that you have an inherent need for adventure in your life. Living in a foreign country fulfills that need like few other things can: exploring new environments, communicating in a different language, learning about local customs and norms, adapting to different climate conditions, and expanding your culinary horizons with local dishes. Your time abroad may also make it easier and more affordable for you to travel to neighboring countries and explore new destinations.

10. **Understanding and Appreciating Home:**

On the other hand, living overseas can deepen your understanding and appreciation of your home country and culture. We often take our upbringing and way of life for granted and only truly grasp our own cultural conditioning when confronted with a different one. There may be aspects of home that we have overlooked or underappreciated, whether it's the infrastructure, nature, our family and friends, or way of life. Going without these things helps us understand and treasure their value.

11. **Enhanced Adaptability and Creativity:**

Moving abroad requires you to reinvent yourself in some ways. As your identity, self-image, and circumstances change, you need to be flexible and open-minded to adapt and thrive. Additionally, you may encounter obstacles and challenges, such as language barriers or cultural differences, that demand creative responses. These skills stay with you and will benefit you in all areas of life.

12. **Unique Educational Opportunities:**

Living in a foreign country can provide unique educational opportunities. Firstly, you may gain access to prestigious universities or centers that you wouldn't have had access to otherwise. Secondly, your experience abroad may prompt or require you to continue your education and learn new skills. On the other hand, especially if you live in a remote area or don't speak the local language fluently, you may be inspired to take advantage of the abundance of online courses available. The more you learn, the more you'll grow, and the more you'll be able to accomplish in life.

13. Improved Problem-Solving Skills:

As a global citizen, you'll likely face challenges that you haven't encountered before, which will encourage you to think outside the box. Consequently, you'll enhance your problem-solving skills, critical thinking, and ability to connect seemingly unrelated dots. These skills are valuable in all aspects of life, and not just while you're abroad. Another clear advantage of leading an international lifestyle!

14. Personal Growth:

Being exposed to new ways of thinking, different cultural practices, and diverse perspectives teaches you a lot about yourself. It also helps you develop new skills and abilities and learn to take care of yourself in unfamiliar situations. Living abroad may also prompt you to seek guidance from a coach, mentor, or experienced confidante, allowing you to gain profound insights into yourself, unfold your potential even under challenging circumstances, and come out stronger on the other side.

15. Making Memories:

They say that today's special moments are tomorrow's memories, and living overseas certainly provides unique opportunities for truly unforgettable experiences! Memories are the building blocks of our identity, emotions, and experiences. Whether you keep them in a journal, photo book, or blog, your memories shape your life story. They allow you to relive past joys, sorrows, and achievements, appreciate your journey, and learn from your mistakes. What would we be without them?

Now I'm curious: What would you add to this list? How has living abroad enriched your life?

H
Helping Hands

If there's one thing I've had to learn while abroad, it's asking for and accepting help. Many women, including myself, often feel compelled to handle everything on their own. This mindset is influenced by societal norms, where women are typically expected to manage household chores, family responsibilities, and the associated mental burden - on top of work and other obligations and activities. There's often an unspoken expectation to excel at 'doing it all'. However, this approach can lead to exhaustion and burnout, especially when we realize that nobody's handing us a badge of honor.

Asking for help is important, but if you're an Expat it becomes a necessity!

If there's a part of you that's reluctant to ask for help, feels uncomfortable doing so or sees it as a sign of weakness, keep reading. Here are 5 compelling reasons why seeking helping hands is crucial!

1. IT'S A PREREQUISITE FOR YOUR LIFE ABROAD

It won't come as a surprise that as a foreigner, there are countless things you are simply unaware of, have difficulty understanding, or can't know: the best places to go (or the ones to avoid), the intricacies of how things work in this country, insider recommendations, and the essential do's and don'ts to bear in mind. The more questions you ask, the more insights you'll gain. And with the help you receive, you'll find yourself accomplishing so much more!

Cultures vary of course, and while in some places, striking up conversations with neighbors, store clerks, and even random people on the street comes naturally, in others, people may be more reserved. Nonetheless, one thing holds true across all cultures: people appreciate being asked for and enjoy sharing their knowledge and expertise. So, what questions do you need to ask to improve your experience abroad? And who can help you with that?

If you're raising children abroad, far from the support of grandparents, aunts, and uncles, it's crucial to seek a network of fellow parents. Connect with others to meet up, exchange impressions, seek advice, or arrange playdates for the kids. Consider the possibility of hiring help or training a reliable babysitter - eventually, you'll find that you need them! Join existing parenting groups or take the initiative to create one yourself. Remember, if it takes a village to raise kids, you're not meant to do it all alone.

2. ASKING FOR HELP REDUCES STRESS AND IMPROVES YOUR WELL-BEING

I know that if you struggle to accept help, it's usually because you care deeply, feel responsible, and want to ensure everything works out perfectly. There might even be a part of you that seeks validation and wants to prove your worth by taking care of everything and everyone.

But trying to do it all takes away the luxury of being fully present and dedicating quality time to what truly matters. It also reduces the joy and ease with which you approach tasks and I believe that's a price we shouldn't pay. Remember: If your good intentions are leaving you exhausted, stressed, and resentful, it's time to reconsider and find better ones!

3. IT ALLOWS YOU TO FOCUS ON YOUR ZONE OF GENIUS

We all possess different skills and talents, and there's so much satisfaction in doing what we're particularly good at. It makes us feel useful, significant, and like we're making a positive impact and difference.

Chances are, you already know your areas of expertise. But just in case you're not fully aware, take a moment to think about what comes effortlessly to you. You know, those things that you do so naturally that they don't even feel like special skills (spoiler alert: they probably are!). What do others notice and praise you for? Where do they come to you for help? What activities bring you so much joy that you completely lose track of time?

If you're a multi-passionate person with many different interests, it may seem like you don't have a clear zone of genius. But in reality, you have several different ones and just need to find a common link to tie them together in some way.

The bottom line is that the more time you have for the things you're good at and that ignite your passion, the better you'll feel, and the more you'll be able to contribute to this world. Keep this in mind the next time you hesitate to delegate or ask for help. It's not that you're incapable or unwilling to do certain things; it's about learning to prioritize what's most important.

4. YOU ENABLE OTHERS TO CONTRIBUTE THEIR EXPERTISE, MAKE A DIFFERENCE OR EARN MONEY

What many of us over-doers and over-givers have in common is that we deeply care about what we do and who we do it for. So how about reframing the situation? Have you ever thought about how you could help someone else by allowing them to help you? By doing so, you enable them to share their expertise, feel useful and significant, or even earn money. It's a win-win situation!

5. YOU FOSTER MEANINGFUL CONNECTIONS

Asking for or offering help is a magical ingredient in building meaningful connections. It creates a sense of closeness, intimacy, and reciprocity that is difficult to achieve otherwise. Expat life can feel lonely and isolated at times, but by joining forces and helping each other out, you can feel significant and connected!

Embracing the power of seeking and accepting help not only lightens our load, it also enriches our lives with valuable connections, newfound opportunities, and a deeper sense of belonging in our community. So, let's lean on each other, share our strengths, and ease the challenges of expat life for one another!

Identity Crisis

One thing many people struggle with when they move abroad is their perceived loss of or change in identity. Have you experienced this too?

You knew exactly who you were (and who you were not) when you lived back home. There were clues all over the place that conveyed a message to yourself and others about your identity: from the family you grew up in, the schools you attended, the people you spent time with, the neighborhood you lived in, and the profession you pursued, among other factors. All of these elements shaped your identity and self-image, thus providing you with a sense of security.

But when you move abroad, these things suddenly lose their meaning. Now, nobody knows about these markers and context anymore. You may no longer continue in the same line of work, and the language barrier might prevent you from fully expressing your personality and knowledge.

Experiencing an identity crisis and feeling misunderstood and insecure is a common consequence. But let me offer you the following reframe:

What if you saw your identity crisis as a once-in-a-lifetime chance to explore a deeper part of yourself, to grow, experiment, and find a sense of authenticity and fulfillment that wasn't available to you before? Imagine it as an opportunity to question and redefine your ideas about what life should be like and who you should be.

During our upbringing, most of us didn't have the luxury of such self-reflection. We were too busy trying to fit in, following rules, and seeking approval from others. Belonging is a basic human need, and when we're young our survival depends on it. To fit in, we often went to great lengths and compromised our authenticity. We made life choices based on what our loved ones, society, or culture expected from us, sometimes without even realizing it. As the years go by, we continue to play roles that we've outgrown and wear labels that were thoughtlessly assigned to us.

What we refer to as our identity is actually just a familiar image of ourselves that we hold onto, believing it will provide us with a sense of belonging, acceptance, and significance.

Realizing that we've been living contrary to our true nature can be a painful experience. It might be a job that initially felt like an accomplishment but takes away our joy, a role in our social circle that no longer resonates, or a life that seems monotonous and predetermined by societal and cultural pressures.

When this happens, we often misinterpret it as a personal failure, feel guilty about not confirming or ashamed about being different. In reality, these realizations, though painful, can actually be transformative moments in our lives, liberating our soul and allowing us to embrace our authentic selves.

That's exactly why having to rethink your old identity, like many expats do, can be a powerful way to explore what else life has to offer and who else you can become.

Remember: Your identity and self-image should serve you, not hold you back from unlocking your full potential and expressing yourself authentically.

So, are you ready to rediscover more of your true self? Then I invite you to think about the following prompts:

- What has always been true about you? What aspects of you have never changed?

- What brings you the most joy? What would you like to experience more of?

- If you had nothing to worry about (money, judgment, childcare etc), how would you love to spend your time?

- What ideas and beliefs do you have about who you should be that don't actually make you feel good at all?

- Which parts of your identity no longer serve you? Who would you like to become instead?

Changing your surroundings can be a wonderful opportunity to explore these questions on your own terms. Enjoy the process!

Keys To Cross-Cultural Confidence

What's invisible, but has the power to make you seen?

It is... your confidence!

Did you know that confidence plays a vital role in our emotional well-being and health? It shapes the lens through which we perceive and respond to the world, giving us a more positive outlook on life and a greater sense of capability and agency.

People with high self-confidence have a secret weapon: they believe in themselves. This belief has a ripple effect on every aspect of their lives. When faced with tricky situations, like conflicts or setbacks, they don't crumble under pressure. Instead, they rise to the occasion with the certainty that they can figure out anything that comes their way. On the other hand, those lacking confidence find it harder to muster the same level of self-assurance, leaving them feeling stuck and unsure of themselves.

Confidence is also closely related to leadership qualities, and those who possess it are better able to draw people in, making them more receptive to their ideas and vision, and consequently to leave their mark. In short, confidence isn't just a nice-to-have quality; it's a game-changer that opens doors to personal and professional satisfaction, success and growth.

THE CULTURE FACTOR

When we become expats, our experience can really shake up our understanding of confidence:

Firstly, a fresh start requires us to start over, oftentimes having to reinvent ourselves in one or more ways. Maybe we've had to switch careers or leave our jobs altogether. We go from effortlessly expressing ourselves in our native language to struggling to communicate even the simplest things. Also, the frequent changes and uncertainties of expat life will put our self-confidence to the test. Adjusting to this new reality takes time, as does embracing it fully.

Furthermore, confidence can be expressed differently in different cultures. What may be seen as confident in one culture could be seen as arrogant or as insecure in another. As expats, we need to first understand and adapt to these cultural differences, and then find our own style that fits our personality, as well as the norms of our new surroundings.

UNLOCKING YOUR CONFIDENCE

Contrary to popular belief, confidence is not an innate trait but a skill that can be learned and mastered. Studies reveal that approximately 50% of confidence is influenced by our genes, but the other 50% is shaped by our environment, experiences, and our personal development.

Therefore, even if you were raised in an environment that didn't prioritize or foster your confidence, you can absolutely acquire it. By embracing new thought patterns, challenging automatic self-doubt, and celebrating your strengths, you can absolutely develop and train your confidence muscles.

One thing that often stands in the way of us feeling confident is our fear of failure. It makes us overthink, second-guess our actions and prevents us from taking risks or seizing opportunities.

But here's a secret: failure is not the enemy of confidence, it's an ally in disguise. Like I said, confidence is a muscle that strengthens through courage and perseverance. If you can learn to embrace failure as a stepping stone to success, you'll not only gain valuable lessons but also discover that the fear of failure is far worse than the failure itself. So, dust yourself off, embrace your imperfections, and let them guide you towards a much more confident version of yourself!

WOMEN AND CONFIDENCE

A great proportion of women grapple with feelings of insecurity and self-doubt. In my coaching practice, confidence is one of the most sought after qualities my clients want to develop. While I'm all for boosting confidence, I also believe that the way this trait has been traditionally defined, heavily influenced by culture and society, isn't inclusive and can lead certain groups of people to doubt themselves. But more on that later.

It's interesting to note that in workplaces, there's a common perception that men are more confident, which often correlates with more frequent promotions and higher salaries. In fact, societal stereotypes play a role in making women appear less sure of themselves, even though they are equally qualified. Studies indicate that men tend to overestimate their abilities and performance, while women tend to underestimate them, despite being equally capable.

Moreover, when men express themselves boldly with clarity and certainty, they often receive positive responses. Women doing the same, on the other hand, frequently encounter criticism. Insights from social psychology research show just how much gender stereotypes shape our expectations and how we interpret the behavior of men and women in society. On top of that, different cultures add extra layers of expectations to the mix, further complicating the picture.

Women often bring a collaborative approach to the workplace, blending empathy and active listening to foster connections while standing their ground. These are undoubtedly valuable leadership skills that enhance teamwork and fuel creativity. And yet, in many male-dominated environments there's still a tendency to prioritize bold displays of confidence, sometimes overshadowing the effectiveness of other approaches.

A NEW TAKE ON CONFIDENCE

It's time to rethink and broaden our understanding of what confidence is, both for ourselves and others. We need to challenge existing norms and appreciate a more inclusive definition that recognizes and celebrates the diverse ways confidence can be expressed - beyond gender stereotypes, cultural differences, and individual personalities.

It was this realization that made me come up with my very own expression of confidence. You see, for the longest time I had thought of myself as lacking boldness, directness and assertiveness. I was everyone's go-to colleague and friend, the one they could always count on, who strived to make others feel at ease and would go with the flow, but never one to impose my will.

When I started my own business, I began thinking about my leadership qualities (or what I thought of as a lack thereof). I read books, articles, and attended seminars on leadership and confidence. Then, during a photo shoot one day, wearing a lace top and a leather jacket, it occurred to me: I had been mistaken all along. I wasn't lacking confidence or leadership qualities at all; my style was simply different from the conventional idea I had in my mind:

My style is soft and flowing like lace. I'm someone who understands different perspectives and empathizes with various ways of being. I believe in the power of team spirit rather than enforcing hierarchies. My confidence doesn't come from strong opinions or dominating heated arguments with others. It comes from my ability to accept and embrace diverse realities without feeling threatened or compelled to abandon my own beliefs.

At the same time, I also have clear values, goals, and standards that represent the firmness of leather. I might avoid conflict and controversy, but I stand my ground and stick to my beliefs.

Lace and Leather. Not either or, but their unique blend. This has become my personal guideline for expressing confidence and leadership skills.

Now, let me ask you: What does your unique expression of confidence look like? How will you need to re-define the concept of confidence in your mind, in order to consciously embrace yours?

J
Juggling Life Between Different Cultures

I personally love getting to know and immersing myself in different cultures. Imagining what my life would be like if I were a local of a different country is one of my favorite mind games. Every profound encounter with a different culture has enriched me, broadened my horizons, and provided me with new ideas, possibilities, and insights. As a fellow global woman, I'm sure you can relate!

Wherever I go, I try to include local dishes in our family menu, incorporate festivities into our calendar, add new songs to my playlists, and include products from different countries in our daily life. But not only that; I've found that the inspiration a global lifestyle offers us can lead to original business ideas, surprising new hobbies, and meaningful, diverse connections.

But being exposed to so many cultural influences also means we'll have to find a way to juggle them all, so they stay alive wherever we go, keep adding value and bringing out the best in us.

In her book, *This Messy Mobile Life*, author Mariam Ottimofiore presents a beautiful metaphor for how different cultural influences shape us, likening it to a *Mola*. A Mola is a hand-stitched, shirt-like piece of clothing from the Guna tribe in South America. It consists of several layers of colored fabric, with some parts exposed and others hidden. Each Mola is unique to the person it was made for. Mariam sees expat life as similar to a Mola. Each destination we move to, and each experience adds another layer that brings out different parts of ourselves. After all, there's a lot we show on the outside, but even more that remains hidden beneath the surface.

The more we allow other cultures to shape us, the less we identify with a single one. Personally, I don't see this as a bad thing. Culture is meant to enrich, not restrict. It should bring people together, not exclude or outcast.

At the same time, cherishing our own heritage, keeping our traditions alive and honoring our roots also goes a long way. Even if you feel like you've somehow outgrown your home culture or that it no longer fully resonates with you, it remains part of your identity. All cultures, even the most misunderstood and misinterpreted, have beautiful traits, stories, flavors, and value.

In my own cross-border life, I've learned to carefully juggle my different cultural influences. Though at times I was focused more on a particular one than another, they've all remained integral parts of me. Despite living abroad and being surrounded by people from around the world in my daily life, I also make it a priority to remain connected with 'home'. In my case, and even though I come from a multicultural family, I have a clear home base - Vienna, Austria - which I know is something not all expats have. Since I'm currently geographically close enough and have the flexibility to do so, I can visit often - another privilege I treasure!

I believe that people represent and bring culture alive more than art, monuments, or music. Maintaining and nurturing my most cherished relationships has kept me grounded, supported, and less alone during difficult times abroad. It also helps me and my children feel closely connected to our city, country, and forging our identities as Global Citizens with Austrian roots.

Which cultures have shaped who you are today? How can you keep them alive and pass them on? And how can you continue to build bridges with the cultural wealth you've been exposed to?

Here are some reflections that have helped me figure this out and successfully juggle my different cultural influences:

Family Tree: Identify the nationalities and cultures in your family tree. Collect stories, memories, pictures, or recipes, and speak to family members about these influences to preserve their richness.

Create Your Unique Cultural Blend: Which countries and cultures have you lived in or traveled to that left a lasting impact on you? What traits, such as lifestyle, language, or celebrations, would you like to take with you? You're probably already doing this somehow, but making a conscious choice about it can provide much clarity and meaning.

Identify your Pallbearers: In some cultures, 6-8 special people carry a loved one's coffin at their funeral. When I heard about this custom, I reflected on who my most important 6-8 people were, aside from family, and how I could remain close to them even over distance.

Who are the special people in your life? I encourage you to write down their names and start nurturing those bonds with particular care, no matter where they are.

Proudly Wear Your Mola: Your cultural background and influences are unique, and you should embrace them with pride. Let's show others the opportunities and benefits that come from opening ourselves up to different influences while also honoring and preserving our heritage.

Loneliness

Loneliness. The L-word. It's painful, dark, and isolating. And it's a completely normal part of expat life.

Firstly, because each move takes you out of your comfort zone. It means saying goodbye to friends and ideally, hello to new acquaintances whom you must first get to know, like, and trust. In some places, you might find it particularly difficult to connect with people, perhaps because there's no international community there or a strong barrier to getting close to the locals.

Humans are social beings with a deep-seated need for belonging and connection. Throughout history, belonging to a tribe or group was integral to our survival, and this inclination remains ingrained in us. In my coaching practice, I've consistently observed that the theme of overcoming loneliness, isolation, or a sense of being different is a common thread among my clients.

When I interviewed Phil McAuliffe (The Lonely Diplomat) for The Empowered Expat Woman Show, he said something beautifully comforting about loneliness, which he calls *a basic human condition*: "Hunger tells us that we need to eat. Thirst tells us that we need to drink. Loneliness tells us that we need connection. That's it."

Experiencing loneliness is completely normal and there's no need to feel ashamed about it. What we need to do is to face the loneliness we feel, look it deep in the eyes, and move through it to come out stronger on the other side. When we learn to better understand what loneliness is and why we feel it, it will lose its grip and power over us. So let's explore where loneliness comes from. If we were to peel back its layers, we'd find the following three sensations at its core:

DISTINCTIVENESS

Feeling distinct and separate from others builds a wall between *you* and *them*. It's pretty much inevitable to stand out as a foreigner, whether it's because of how you look, your accent, or cultural differences. Your uniqueness might make you feel like you're on a separate wavelength from everyone else, which makes it difficult to attain that feeling of fitting in.

INADEQUACY

Inadequacy can show up in different ways. For instance, have you ever compared yourself to others and wondered, "Why am I having such a hard time here? Why don't things work out more easily for me?" This comparison and following disappointment can leave you with a lingering feeling that something might be inherently wrong with you.

There's another aspect to inadequacy as well. Some expats report feeling 'less than' the people in their host countries, especially if they consider those countries more advanced than their own or face negative cultural stereotypes related to their heritage.

At other times, feeling 'more privileged' than the locals can bring on discomfort and a sense of intrusion. Both of these scenarios also contribute to feelings of inadequacy, which again, stand in the way of fostering real connections and belonging.

FEAR

Everyone has a certain fear of rejection and craves belonging and acceptance. Moving abroad can be scary, making us feel vulnerable, awkward, and dependent. Moreover, women who move abroad long-term often fear losing their identity, or are concerned that one day they'll find they've made the wrong decision. Whatever your fear may be, it can stand in the way of fully letting your guard down and embracing your status quo.

Can you identify what roles these three elements play in your life abroad? What exactly is perpetuating your sense of loneliness?

When you can pinpoint these factors, give your vague feelings and fleeting thoughts a name and understand what led to them, it becomes much easier to address and manage them.

Now the question remains: what can we do to combat loneliness?

Self-Awareness:

It's tempting to distract yourself from unpleasant feelings. What do you typically do to get your mind off of them?

The thing is, our feelings won't just go away; in fact, they often intensify when we try to push them aside. A more effective approach is to confront them head-on and become familiar with them. By recognizing how loneliness shows up in your life and impacts you, you can identify it more quickly and take steps to improve your well-being.

Connecting with Others:

Humans are naturally wired for connection. When you move to a foreign country, it requires some additional effort to establish relationships. I encourage you to be friendly, show genuine interest in people, give them the benefit of the doubt, take initiative and be open to saying 'yes' to plans. If that feels challenging, offering your help to someone is another great way to connect. There's always someone you can assist.

Don't forget to maintain and nurture connections with your loved ones back home or at a previous destination. Knowing that there are people who love you, even if they're far away, will give you a strong sense of comfort, security and emotional relief in times of loneliness.

Connecting with Yourself:

Being your own best friend, your biggest ally, and tapping into your 'Inner Happy Place' becomes even more important when you have to start from scratch in a new country. How can you fill your own emotional bucket? How can you be kind, loving, and nurturing to yourself? What can you do for yourself to feel better in times of loneliness?

Authenticity:

When you truly know yourself and aren't afraid to be genuine, you increase your chances of finding real belonging. Sometimes, we try so hard to fit in, in order to be accepted by a group. But if it means hiding who you truly are and what you believe in, you won't ever feel like you truly belong because you're not being yourself to begin with.

Others might pick up on your lack of authenticity, leading them to keep their distance or not fully open up to you either. To build strong connections with yourself and others, take the time to understand who you are and always be true to yourself.

Community:

This is similar to connection but takes it a step further. Being part of a community is what makes a place feel like 'home' for many. Can you find a community based on shared interests or other commonalities? Most cities have expat or international women's clubs, as well as networking groups. If you have children, you can connect with parents at school and participate in activities there. Maybe there's a sport or hobby you enjoy where you can join a team or group and connect with like-minded people.

Community creates a sense of belonging and combats loneliness. So, while it may take a little longer to establish, it's one powerful antidote to feeling alone and isolated!

By applying these strategies, you can effectively address and combat loneliness in your expat life. You got this!

Making A Home Away From Home

They say there's no place like home... but sometimes, our busy lives and short-term leases can make us forget to make our place feel like it.

Over the years, and throughout many moves, I've seen firsthand what a difference it makes to enjoy being in a comfortable, pleasant and safe environment you can call home. Here are 10 of my favorite tips to achieve that!

1. **Unpack immediately**

    Living between boxes is stressful and makes the beginnings in a new country even harder. Everything is foreign enough as it is, but having a cozy home and a place to retreat to will give you a lot of comfort! Take advantage of the momentum of a move, so that you don't get used to things being half-done.

2. **Decorate your space**

    No matter how long or short the stay, decorate your home as if you were there for the long haul! To do so, you don't necessarily need to spend a lot of money. You can make your place cozy by hanging up pictures, filling the closets, and allocating a few statement pieces. Use warm lighting, comfortable seating, and cozy textiles to create a welcoming atmosphere in your home.

I always like to start with the most important room, so that even if it takes a little longer to fully arrange the others, you have one sacred space set up quickly! I usually start with the kids' rooms because I presume moving to a different home is hardest on them. Which room is most important to you? Where do you spend the most time?

3. **Personalize your home**

   Whenever possible, bring your favorite furniture and decorative items with you to create a sense of continuity and familiarity in your (globally mobile) home. By mixing elements like furniture, decor, and styles from the different cultures and countries that have influenced you, you will create a unique style and space over the years! Overall, choose pieces that reflect your personality, experiences, and style. That way, your new home will feel like it's truly 'yours'.

4. **Photos**

   Unfortunately, we can't pack our parents, friends, etc., in our suitcases or moving trucks. But they can still smile at you through a photograph that'll bring back fond memories and cheer you up when you feel low.

5. **Your happy place**

   Find a corner in your 'home away from home' that you particularly like and make it your personal happy place. To anchor feel-good vibes to this corner, engage in your favorite activities there, and keep it clean and cared for.

6. **Feng Shui**

   I once took a Feng Shui course, and since then, I can't get these concepts out of the back of my mind. When setting up our current and previous homes, I took the lucky Feng Shui directions and fundamental teachings into account. I encourage you to give it a try!

7. **Want mail?**

    Getting mail may be old-fashioned, but who doesn't love to receive a letter or holiday greeting delivered to your door? Memorize your new address and share it with friends around the world.

8. **The kitchen**

    Keeping a stock of your favorite ingredients from home (or elsewhere) that are hard to find locally can be a source of comfort when you're in need of familiar foods! Bring them with you, order them online, or find a local seller. The kitchen is a place of nourishment, encounter, and togetherness, so try to create an atmosphere that reflects that.

9. **Get to know your surroundings**

    Explore your new neighborhood and discover what your block has to offer. What stores, restaurants, or other amenities can you find there? Is there a shortcut to your home or to a place of interest? How do you get from your house to others'? Be friendly with your neighbors, store clerks, and waiters at the places you frequent. This will help you feel more connected to your local community and like you're part of it.

10. **Host a housewarming party or dinner**

    If you've already made some friends in your host country, inviting them over can be a key step in making yourself feel more at home. A housewarming gathering doesn't only mark your official residence but hopefully also leads to future invitations from your guests, and the opportunity to further expand your social circle.

Networking And Socializing Abroad

One thing all of us expats have in common when we move to a new place is our need to build a personal and professional network there - oftentimes from scratch.

When it comes to meeting people, you might encounter different cultural rules and norms. Some cultures seem more open, welcoming, and friendly, while in others, it's hard to strike up a conversation and get close to people. I've experienced both and found that the way locals initially engage with strangers and foreigners doesn't necessarily determine the quality of friendships you'll be able to make.

In fact, it's often in those cultures where people seem more reserved, serious, and less approachable that very profound and long-lasting friendships are made. So, regardless of the cultural environment you find yourself in, don't jump to conclusions, and don't give up too quickly.

Here are a few of my favorite tips for finding new friends and building your network abroad:

BE INTRODUCED

Getting a friend or acquaintance to introduce you to people in your new country can grant you access to a community of potentially like-minded individuals. As a bonus, this referral creates a greater sense of commitment and consideration towards you, so they won't see you as a complete stranger but as a mutual friend. Who do you know who's currently living in your new host country, who's originally from there, or who used to live there? If no one comes to mind, ask your friends and colleagues if they know anybody from there.

When you get a contact, reach out to them. While it may feel a bit strange to approach someone you don't really know, people generally love sharing their knowledge, tips, and advice. Plus, they'll want you to have a positive experience in their country or the country they know well. It wouldn't be surprising if they offered to meet you once you get there or put you in contact with somebody who will.

After that first contact, make sure to stay in touch - let them know when you arrive or send them a little thank-you note when you try that restaurant they recommended. Staying top of their mind ensures that they'll think of you and invite you on another occasion.

Most of my best friendships abroad have been made possible thanks to a common link, so I'm sure this approach can have a similar impact on you.

BECOME AN ACTIVE MEMBER OF A COMMUNITY

Whether it's an expat club, your kid's school or class, a sports club, book club, or religious group - join it! Ideally, it should be a community where you'll actually interact with people and won't remain anonymous (like you may in a gym).

Community creates belonging, which is something we all strive for, especially when we move abroad. But community also creates connections, synergies, possibilities, and opportunities you wouldn't have otherwise.

If you can't find a community in your area, think about creating your own club. I've had clients start their own expat communities, book clubs and workout groups - there are always people looking to connect with like-minded others, so be proactive about finding your tribe! Social media and meet up apps can help you connect with people if you don't know many locally.

BECOME A PEOPLE MAGNET

Especially in your first months after arriving in a new destination (or in the weeks following your reading this book) I encourage you to make an effort to do the following:

- **Talk to everyone:** Be friendly to your neighbors, the store-clerk, the waiter at the coffee shop, other parents at the park, your colleagues at work - whether they're subordinates or superiors. If you're open-minded, warm, and welcoming, it will come back to you. Doing this will also make you naturally feel more connected, which is an attractive energy to be in!

- **Take an honest interest in people:** Even in the ones that don't really seem to interest you. After all, this is about growing your network, and you never know who this person may introduce you to. Or they may surprise you and turn out to be a great friend after all! As a coach, I witness firsthand how thirsty people are to be listened to and taken an interest in. We all want to feel seen and heard, and if you can make someone feel that way, they will remember you for it! They will feel grateful and more obliged to you - and that's how another connection is born.

- **Offer your help:** If you're an introvert or simply shy, this pro tip is for you. Think about where or whom you could help - spoiler alert: there's always someone in need of support! What do you know that would be of value to someone else? Who around you is in need and would be grateful for your helping hands? This is another great way to build a bond with someone, that doesn't require 'putting yourself out there'!

BE PROACTIVE ABOUT NETWORKING

They say your network is your net worth. If you're in business, you need to focus on yours! Reach out to local business associations or your home country's chamber of commerce, and attend relevant trade shows and conferences.

Networking events are another great way to meet people and build business relationships in your new country. Make sure to have a compelling pitch - possibly translated into the local language and memorized perfectly!

Depending on your profession or company, you could also consider working with a local partner. Exploring synergies and collaborations can be a very effective way to get a foothold and build a network abroad. Look for local organizations or businesses that cater to your target audience and share your goals and values.

While it takes some initial effort on your part and consistency, it's absolutely possible to build and grow your personal and professional network abroad. Following these tips will get you there sooner than later!

Owning Who You Are

As Expat Women living a crossborder lifestyle, our lives look very different to that of others. The more places and people we get to know, the more we broaden our horizons to what else is possible. By witnessing different ways of life, we're gifted with the ability to look at things differently and make choices we didn't know we had before.

As you try to balance staying true to yourself while wholeheartedly embracing new influences, you start crafting your own unique cross-cultural identity, lifestyle, and circumstances.

This doesn't always make life easier though, especially if you're still trying to 'find your place', compare yourself to non-nomads, or second-guess your choices and decisions.

In this chapter let's explore how you can fully embrace your unique path, by owning who you are, where you're at and where you're going.

OWNING WHERE YOU'RE FROM

It always pains me to see when people hide or lie about their heritage, refrain from speaking their mother tongue in public or talk badly about their home country. Of course, your constructive criticism about your country of origin has its place and it's not healthy to tie your identity too strongly to a country or culture.

But rejecting your origins can mean rejecting a part of yourself. It's important to make peace with who you are and where you come from - even when you feel that you've outgrown that identity or if you strongly disagree with politicians and certain developments. If you have a multicultural background, you get to embrace all of the influences, at least to the different degrees they've shaped you.

I recently read my dad's memoir, where he shared stories, memories, and interesting facts about our family lineage. One particular figure who captivated my attention was my Italian great-grandfather, a globally-minded entrepreneur I never had the chance to meet in person, but immediately felt connected to, nevertheless.

In a way, connecting with our ancestors can evoke that sense of belonging to something greater - a feeling so many expats yearn for. It also provides valuable context to our upbringing, helping us understand the influences, traumas, and values passed down through the generations that shape who we are today.

Owning where you're from isn't just about embracing your heritage; it's about honoring the journey that brought you here and the legacy that continues to shape your identity. By acknowledging and embracing your roots, you can find strength, resilience, and a deeper sense of belonging amidst relocations and life changes.

EMBRACE YOUR DISTINCTIVENESS

Many foreigners will face negative stereotypes or even hostility related to our heritage. Remember, you're not responsible for your country's history, politics, crime rates, or cultural traits. In fact, by proudly being yourself, you might be the one who changes other's limited perception of your heritage.

Unfortunately, there are also people who are simply too narrow-minded to see beyond their prejudices. Hopefully you can avoid their company because, as a global woman, they clearly do not share your values and experiences!

The bottomline is that you don't need to prove your worth and value to anyone. The more confident and accepting you are of your story, the better you will be able to stand your ground, keep looking forward and continue on your path.

Being different is not a weakness, it's your asset! I like to think of us expats as 'ambassadors of diversity' - now that's an empowering reframe of being the perpetual outsider, don't you think?

Think about your unique skills, talents and experiences, and use them to your advantage. Whether it's your language skills, your creativity, or your ability to adapt to new situations. Always remember that you have something valuable to say and contribute. You bring a different perspective to the table, and the world is in need of that!

BEWARE OF THE COMPARISON TRAP

They say comparison is the thief of joy, and I'm sure you've experienced how it can affect your self-esteem in a new culture, just like I have.

On the one hand, you compare yourself to your friends back home who seem to have steady lives, pursuing goals you were taught were worth pursuing, living the life you could have lived had you not moved abroad.

But on the other hand, you also compare yourself to your new local friends and colleagues, aware of the expectations in your host country as you navigate cultural differences. Trying to live up to local cultural expectations may make you feel somewhat inadequate because your background and past have shaped your values, views, and character differently.

Here's the thing: constantly comparing yourself to others is a never-ending cycle that only leads to self-doubt and frustration. It's time to break free from the comparison trap and start looking inward for validation and direction. Instead of seeking external validation, you need to become your own compass and chart your own unique path.

BE A TRENDSETTER

One thing's for certain: our individuality is like a fresh breath of air that can bring something unique and special to any table.

I'm always in awe of celebrities who captivate our attention, simply by fully embracing and proudly flaunting their distinctiveness. They're able to make certain traits, looks, or styles trendy and cool, even if they weren't before, just by radiating confidence and being true to who they are. It's their unapologetic uniqueness that draws us in like a magnet.

As diverse, globally-minded Expat Women, we have the power to do the same - and so we really should! Instead of striving to be like others, let's proudly celebrate our authentic, layered selves and become trendsetters for what we stand for. By embracing our distinctiveness, we not only inspire others but also create a ripple effect of self-acceptance and empowerment for others.

So let's unleash our inner trendsetters and confidently show the world the power of being true to ourselves! What makes you 'you'? What do you stand for? What are your distinctive skills, talents, and experiences?

Embracing your unique qualities will boost your confidence and empower you to make a positive impact, wherever you are.

Power Of Words

Words have an incredible influence over us, whether they're spoken out loud or quietly thought to ourselves. Have you noticed how your self-talk, the conversations you have in your mind, sometimes runs unchecked and on autopilot? Or how people choose exaggerated words for dramatic effect, to entertain their friends?

Here's the issue: Each word you choose carries a world of meaning, shaped by culture, society, and your own life story. As these words echo in your mind, they craft a compelling narrative that your subconscious absorbs, shaping how you perceive the world and how you respond to it.

When you casually throw around phrases like 'I'm devastated' or 'What a tragedy!', your brain's limbic system springs into action. It interprets these words as stress signals, setting off a chain reaction in your body. You may notice your body tensing up, your breath becoming shallow, or changes in your appetite.

The words we use don't just impact how we feel - they also shape our perspective of the world. Stick to a negative script, and you'll reinforce negative neural pathways in your brain, heightening your sensitivity to life's challenges and causing you to anticipate, notice, and focus on them more.

On the other hand, embracing positive and empowering words flips the script entirely. Your brain rewards you with a surge of feel-good chemicals like dopamine and serotonin. That's why it's crucial to take a step back and reflect on the words you use and the stories you tell yourself. Are they harming you or empowering you?

Understanding the profound influence of words on our biology allows us to take control of our inner dialogue. This newfound awareness empowers us to select words that inspire and energize us, rather than feeding into negativity. By consciously reshaping the stories we tell ourselves, we can forge new neural pathways, fostering a mindset of resilience and positivity.

CHOOSE YOUR WORDS WISELY

Personally, I'm a real advocate for using words with precision, whether we're talking to ourselves or others. My grandfather, a seasoned diplomat, was a master at articulating his thoughts with careful consideration. Growing up, I always admired how he steered clear of vague expressions, simplifications, or exaggerations. His meticulous attention to detail could seem intimidating at first, but actually, it was so liberating and reassuring to be around someone who wouldn't be swayed by sensationalist, biased or moody views. In a world where simplifications and biases often dominate the media and dictate arguments, a commitment to using nuanced, discerning language is priceless!

Speaking of expressing ourselves with care, did you know that we only use a small fraction of the vocabulary available to us in any language? This also applies when describing our emotional state, often leading to vague approximations. For example, if you frequently feel 'angry', it's worth reflecting on whether you might actually be experiencing annoyance, disappointment, frustration, embarrassment, vulnerability, or something else?

Take the time to reflect on your feelings and get to know your reactions better. By choosing the most precise words to describe what you're experiencing, you not only gain insight into your emotions but also foster a deeper sense of self-awareness and inner peace.

ASK BETTER QUESTIONS

The questions you ask yourself have a profound impact on the quality of your life. Just imagine what difference it would make to replace questions like "Why can't I achieve this?" or "Why does this always happen to me?" with more empowering alternatives.

For instance, asking "What three things can I do right now (or stop doing) that would help me achieve this?" or "How can I ensure that this doesn't happen to me again?" immediately opens up more creative ways of thinking, as well as new possibilities and outlooks.

By asking yourself truly insightful questions, you not only enhance your overall well-being, but you also unlock new resources and opportunities in your life. So take a moment to reflect on the questions that typically fill your mind, especially during challenging times. How can you rephrase them in more empowering terms?

After all, you have the power to transform your life abroad into an extraordinary journey of self-discovery and growth simply by harnessing the power of your words and asking better questions.

Queen Energy

Did you know that growing up my biggest dream was to become a famous singer? I would spend hours and hours writing and recording songs, rehearsing choreographies or practicing (fictional) interviews.

At 17, I let a renowned music producer burst my bubble. Back in those days before YouTube, when you had to be 'discovered.' He gave me some harsh feedback I couldn't handle at the time about 'not being special': not my voice, not my songs, not my looks.

I still remember sitting there, trying to act cool as he went on and on about my un-specialness and seemingly delusional dreams. On the inside I felt like he was ripping my heart out. I left the meeting with my head hanging low and although I continued making music for several more years, I never again viewed 'becoming a singer' as something I could pursue.

And yet, this experience left a mark on me, for two reasons:

On the one hand, thinking of my teenage self sitting there and allowing the harsh feedback of a 40-something year old detractor to shatter my self-belief and confidence, still makes me angry. Because the only thing worse than someone walking all over you is letting them. That day, I vowed to never let anyone make me feel worthless again. I still have a low tolerance for unkindness and disrespect.

On the other hand, this experience made me develop a strong desire to be an uplifting, motivating and kind force for others, helping them tap into their dreams and unfold their potential. Success isn't solely determined by our gifts and talents; it's the passion, originality, and grit with which we pursue our goals that ultimately lead to outstanding results! There isn't just one path to success. Everyone is on their own unique journey and can make a positive impact in their own special way.

UNLEASH YOUR QUEEN WITHIN

Having big dreams and the courage to chase them demands high self-esteem, a dash of audacity, and courage. Reflecting on my past, I realize that my years of dreaming about fame and practicing MTV Music Awards acceptance speeches made me normalize and embrace those qualities. They helped me develop what I now refer to as 'Queen Energy', an attribute that I believe Empowered Expat Women should embody!

The Queen is a powerful archetype that embodies feminine strength, sovereignty, and leadership. A queen is regal, dignified, confident, and powerful. The archetype of the queen can be found in many cultures, usually representing female power.

Tapping into your queen energy can help you feel more confident, empowered, and capable of leading in all areas of your life. Whether you're an expat executive or entrepreneur, an accompanying spouse, a student abroad, or a stay-at-home mom, queen energy can help you unfold your inner strength and take your life into your own hands.

So, how can you tap into your queen energy? Here are a few ways:

KNOW YOUR WORTH

Queens value themselves highly. They are confident in their abilities and don't let anyone else determine their worth. You can strengthen your sense of self-worth by making the relationship with yourself a priority:

Make an effort to get to know yourself fully. Take time to explore your thoughts. Allow yourself to feel your feelings. Observe when you feel good and when not - and why not? Most importantly, pay attention to the many things that make you worthy, valuable and lovable. You have an absolute right to exist, to take up space and to be who you are - on your good days and bad days.

To increase your own sense of self-worth it's also important to set goals and commit to achieving them. Once you've determined that a goal is important, don't let yourself down or make excuses for why you can't do what you've committed to.

But no matter what happens, treat yourself with loving kindness. As the queen that you are, you deserve to be treated with the utmost respect - and it starts with yourself!

SET BOUNDARIES

Queens are excellent at setting boundaries and enforcing them. They have high standards, know what they want and what they will not tolerate.

Boundaries allow us to assign responsibilities and regulate what's okay and what's not okay, both emotionally or physically. They show you where you end and another person begins, so that you don't take responsibility for what's theirs (like their bad mood, their limiting beliefs, their insecurity or rudeness). When you don't set good boundaries it will often come to the detriment of your mental or physical health. It also negatively affects your relationships - both, with others and with yourself.

Remember: You are allowed to create your own boundaries and standards AND to enforce them!

LEAD BY EXAMPLE

Queens don't just talk the talk, they walk the walk. They set a positive example and live their life with integrity. To achieve this, you will need to be true to yourself, your values, and priorities.

Pay attention to the actions you take and the decisions you make. Stand for something. Whether you know it or not, you are a role model to others, so don't take the impact you can have on them lightly!

EMBRACE YOUR FEMININITY

Queens are not afraid to embrace their femininity. They are strong, powerful, and confident - in a feminine way. Because of our patriarchal past and structures, many of us still believe that so-called feminine traits are 'weak' and that in order to be strong and successful, you need to be 'more like a man'.

As an Empowered Expat Woman you know this couldn't be further from the truth. So let's boldly redefine femininity on our terms, fully expressing ourselves and celebrate our womanhood! After all, femininity is a formidable source of power in its own right.

Rock Bottom Abroad (And How To Rise From It)

We've all been there, right? Those moments of frustration and weariness that just leave us feeling drained. Hitting rock bottom while living abroad can be an especially tough pill to swallow, making you feel even more alone and isolated.

When you reach such a low point, it's important to remember that you can't simply expect yourself to snap out of it in the blink of an eye. The emotions and struggles you're facing are often the result of underlying issues that have been simmering below the surface for some time. Distractions and false positivity won't magically make them go away.

So, instead, let me walk you through a process that will help you cope and rise stronger than before. But before we dive in, let's look at what we might gain from these low moments abroad.

UNCOVERING HIDDEN GAINS

Setbacks, disappointments, and emotional turmoil require immense inner strength to overcome. The journey to rock bottom is often a culmination of various factors that have slowly been draining your energy, resilience, and optimism over time. Mustering up this strength might seem impossible, making dwelling in sadness a seemingly comfortable alternative.

You see, allowing yourself to be sad or depressed can actually help you connect with yourself. It's like pressing pause on the chaos of life, giving yourself permission to slow down and listen inward. What's more, you often receive empathetic support from loved ones who reach out more frequently or offer thoughtful gestures to lift your spirits. It's often in these vulnerable times that we start to humbly appreciate the things and people we have in our life, which is a good thing.

Another hidden gain of dwelling in sadness is the permission to cut yourself some slack. Maybe you now feel justified to say "no" to annoying commitments or appointments and choose to indulge in your favorite show instead. Or you might treat yourself to another piece of cake or a new purse.

These low moments offer a much-needed opportunity for connection, both with yourself and with others. And yet, it's important to see that this connection comes from a place of disempowerment, helplessness, or self-pity. While it might provide temporary relief, it's not the kind of connection or attention that ultimately feels fulfilling or empowering.

RISING FROM THE ASHES

In these rock-bottom moments, seeing the light at the end of the tunnel can be challenging. But by following these 3 steps, you can find your way out of the darkness:

STEP 1: ACCEPT

The first step is acceptance. Acknowledge that you have reached rock bottom and recognize that it's okay to be there.

You can trust in your ability to endure and overcome this stage, just as you have endured and overcome previous challenges. We often fear facing our unpleasant feelings, worrying that it will only deepen our pain or make it harder to recover. But actually, it's the act of suppressing or denying our pain that truly makes us feel bad and alone.

There's no shame in admitting, "I'm struggling. I can't go on. This isn't how I imagined my life or a situation to be." We must mourn what isn't, what wasn't, and what won't be. Yes, this is painful, sad, and overwhelming. It's also an essential part of the healing process.

By allowing ourselves to fully feel these unsettling emotions, we create a safe space for ourselves to just *be*, in the midst of the turmoil. We also create space for transformation.

Just make sure you don't dwell in this state for too long, as this can form and foster unhealthy habits, negative or fatalistic thinking, chronic worry, victimhood, or depression. I encourage you to seek support from a trained professional who can provide guidance during this stage.

STEP 2: REFRAME

There is so much power in reframing a difficult situation. Clever reframes allow us to shift our focus and find a new lens through which to view a situation.

As the great Viktor Frankl pointed out, humans have an incredible capacity to endure hardships when they can find a sense of meaning in them. This allows us to make sense of what seemed incomprehensible before, and we can uncover hidden opportunities, lessons, or silver linings we were unable to see before.

My favorite reframe, which has helped me move through challenges, goes as follows: Instead of viewing moments of disappointment, frustration, and pain as dead-ends, see them as opportunities for a U-turn, an escape route from a mediocre life or an unfulfilling situation. Thank goodness for those moments, without which we'd just keep going down the wrong path!

After some time of sadness and grief, embrace the notion that everything happens for a reason and that countless possibilities exist for our lives, even if we can't currently see or consider them. Sometimes, we must reach rock bottom to start searching for new paths. When we surrender control and trust in our ability to recover, the accumulated tension can finally be released.

STEP 3: RELEASE & TRANSFORM

In this phase, let me introduce you to a coaching tool I created called 'The Ambivalent Letter'. It's an exercise that allows you to release the pain and gradually, gently, and naturally transform it.

Here's how it works: On a sheet of paper, write down everything you hate about your current situation. Give yourself 10 minutes or so to go on an unapologetic rant; feel free to exaggerate, even shout out the words as you write them - don't hold back, you want to let it all out!

When you feel that you've written out everything you had to say and that you feel a little lighter after blowing off steam, take a few deep breaths. Then, go on to explore a different side of the story and reflect on what about the situation makes you sad, disappointed, or insecure. Allowing yourself to be vulnerable will not only help you to better understand the complexity of the situation but will also soften you.

Finally, end this letter on a more empowered note: Write out what you wish for yourself, what you would need to improve the situation, and potential new perspectives you hadn't yet considered. You may even come up with a thing or two you've learned (or will learn) through hitting rock bottom and manage to feel grateful for that.

No matter what you're going through, this tool will make you feel seen, heard, and comforted, while guiding you to move towards the light at the end of the tunnel. It may take time to reach that light, and that's perfectly okay. Trust that when you emerge, you will be stronger, wiser, and clearer about what you want for yourself.

To get the most out of this exercise, download your free, fillable template for 'The Ambivalent Letter' from www.camillaquintana.com/book.

Remember, hitting rock bottom abroad doesn't mean it's the end. It's the beginning of a transformation and a new chapter in your life. Acknowledge the pain, honor your feelings, and trust in your resilience. After all, you have the power to rise, thrive, flourish and make the most of your life abroad!

Self-Care Strategies For Exhausting Times Abroad

In our fast-paced lives filled with countless responsibilities and limited time to unwind, finding moments of self-care can be especially challenging.

As an expat or foreigner, you might face additional obstacles such as having to adapt to a new culture, dealing with homesickness, or feeling isolated from familiar support networks. Navigating daily tasks in a different language can also be stressful, as well as feeling the pressure to prove yourself and keep up with local colleagues and friends.

For parents living abroad, the challenges multiply. Raising children away from home without the support of extended family or close friends can be overwhelming. Balancing childcare responsibilities with work or other commitments adds another layer of complexity, leaving little time for personal relaxation or self-care.

In my personal experience, raising three children away from home has often left me feeling like the sole go-to person, responsible for meeting their needs and compensating for the absence of relatives or close family friends nearby. An added challenge was the fact that my husband was frequently away for work, leaving me to shoulder much of the parenting responsibilities alone. Add to that the demands of managing a growing business and navigating months of lockdowns and holidays...

Though in theory I knew how important self-care was, especially in stressful times, there often simply was no time for that. Wanting to carve it out felt like 'yet another thing' I had to do. It felt really frustrating, because my expectation of what self-care should look like (as seen on social media) was so different from my reality.

It was around this time that I started experimenting with possible ways to nurture myself, under the most chaotic and restrictive circumstances. Let me tell you how that went!

The first thing I came up with that granted me tremendous relief was a concept I named:

MICRO-MOMENTS OF SELF-CARE

These moments are not defined by the amount of time you have available, but by the intention you have to connect with yourself and to replenish.

There's so much power and peace in consciously deciding to simply make a given moment truly special and just about you, instead of either rushing through it or daydreaming about a magic wand to make your stress and stressors go away (been there, done that!).

Though they might initially seem insignificant, these micro-moments can be essential for mental well-being during truly hectic times.

Such a micro-moment of self-care could be:

- Peacefully sipping your cup of coffee at your favorite spot in your home.

- Taking an extra long shower (with your favorite products, music or a scented candle)
- Combining something you have to do (e.g. chores) with something you love to do (e.g. listening to a podcast)
- Singing and dancing to your favorite song
- A 5-minute mindfulness or deep breathing exercise
- Lying down with a 10-minute guided power nap meditation
- Unwinding with a body check, by scanning and feeling into every part of your body, from toes to head
- Hold a restorative yoga pose (e.g. child pose) for a couple of minutes
- Asking yourself one powerful question and reflecting or journaling about it

When life gets overwhelmingly busy, it's essential to integrate small, nurturing gestures that require minimal time, preparation, or effort into your daily routine. I encourage you to consciously dedicate a few of those non-negotiable 3-10 minute slots to your own nourishment each day.

CREATING THE RIGHT CONDITIONS FOR SELF-CARE

Another significant challenge that made it difficult for me to prioritize self-care during busy times was related to my circumstances and habits. When you're in desperate need to unwind and recharge your batteries, creating the right conditions for yourself to achieve that can work wonders! Here's how:

1. Limit Screen Time

Our smartphones have become almost like an extension of ourselves: we always carry them around and rely on them for a myriad of things. As you read these lines, it's very likely that your phone is lying next to you, drawing your attention to it with every beep and vibration it makes. Our constant availability, coupled with the expectation to always be responsive, can become a significant source of stress. It can also prevent us from deeply connecting and engaging with other people, effectively completing our tasks, or savoring special moments.

Many women also feel pressured by social media, whether it's keeping up with posting and commenting, falling into the dangerous comparison trap when viewing others' seemingly perfect lives, or simply spending excessive time mindlessly scrolling (only to regret it later).

I know how tempting it is to use your phone as a means to unwind. However, more often than not, excessive screen time is not the best or most sustainable way to achieve relaxation. In fact, it may even be detrimental to your ability to replenish yourself. Here are a few reasons why:

- The blue light emitted by screens can disrupt our circadian rhythm, making it harder to fall asleep at night.

- Many screen activities are designed to keep us constantly stimulated and engaged, to the point of becoming addicted.

- Excessive screen time promotes sedentary behavior, which can lead to feeling fatigue or restlessness.

- Let's not forget the information overload we receive through our phones, making it difficult to switch off and disconnect from the world.

I am certainly not trying to demonize our phones because I, too, am grateful for everything I can do thanks to this little device. The key is to remain consciously in control of our phone usage, rather than letting it control us.

2. Cognitive Load

When I first learned about this concept from one of my mentors, I didn't really understand and therefore disregarded it. But as I delved deeper into the topic, I started to see how much it affected my well-being, peace of mind, and ability to relax.

Cognitive load refers to the amount of mental effort required to complete a task or process information. Imagine it like your brain's workload. When you have too much to think about all at once, such as trying to focus on different things, juggling several tasks, or dealing with an overwhelming amount of information, it becomes hard to concentrate, think clearly - or to disconnect.

The mental load experienced by mothers has rightfully gained attention as a significant topic, serving as a reference point here. Let's explore what else adds to our cognitive load:

- **Information Overload:** In today's world, we are bombarded with endless inputs from various sources. Our brains struggle to process and filter all the incoming information, leading to cognitive overload, mental exhaustion, anxiety, and stress.

- **Unfinished Business:** Every time we set out to do something but don't complete it for whatever reason, we leave an 'open loop' in our brain. Even if we postpone and forget about these tasks eventually, they continue to linger in our subconsciousness. All of these open loops, whether we're aware of them or not, occupy mental space, and that makes it difficult for our brains to enter a state of true relaxation. That's why it's important to consciously drop or postpone these unfinished tasks, in order to allow our brain to release them from its working memory (at least for the time being).

- **Multitasking:** Have you ever prided yourself on being a great multitasker? This skill is often attributed to women, but unfortunately for us, studies on multitasking have shown that when our brains are unable to fully focus on any one task, it decreases our performance, accuracy, and retention. It also leaves us feeling overwhelmed and overstimulated. To reduce cognitive load, it's better to prioritize one task at a time and consciously focus on seeing it through.

- **Expat Life:** As an expat, I consider our lifestyle another factor that adds to our cognitive load. In my multilingual life, I often find myself processing different people speaking to me simultaneously in different languages. For example, I might be listening to an English audiobook or podcast while my children are speaking to me in German, and my husband drops in with a request in Spanish. Additionally, the need to memorize numerous new things, from foreign names to codes of conduct or directions, requires mental effort.

To cope with and reduce cognitive load, try to set better boundaries related to the points mentioned above. It's also advisable to write your to-do list down instead of relying solely on your brain. Finally, forgive yourself for the things you haven't been able or willing to do. Even if they are things you consider irrelevant, take a moment to officially let them go, so that your brain can release them from its working memory.

3. Get Enough Sleep

Did you know this is the ultimate act of self-care? We often view sleep as unproductive or a waste of time when we have a lot to do, leading us to reduce the hours we spend sleeping. In fact, sleep is the most productive and regenerative activity for our minds and bodies. It improves our mood, mental functioning, and overall well-being.

Some people pride themselves on being able to function on 5 or 6 hours of sleep, but numerous studies have shown the detrimental consequences this can have on our health. It, for instance, increases the risk of depression, diabetes, obesity, dementia, accidents, high blood pressure, and various other health issues. It has even been said to reduce lifespan by three years (and just think about what you could do with those!).

So, even if you think you don't need much sleep, imagine how much better you could feel and function with an extra hour or two.

4. Accelerated Deep Relaxation Techniques

I'm a big fan of these techniques and exercises, as they're specifically designed to effectively lower stress, improve mental performance, and recharge energy.

One of my go-to techniques is Binaural Beats: Through your headphones, you receive two different tones in each ear, which your brain compensates by creating a third frequency, known as a binaural beat. As your brain synchronizes its brain waves to these frequencies, you can enter a different state of mind. The alpha (α) pattern induces relaxation and creativity, the theta (θ) pattern leads to a meditative state, and the delta (δ) pattern is associated with deeper sleep stages and healing.

Other powerful deep relaxation techniques I like to do include guided power nap meditations, meditation itself, Yin Yoga, deep breathing techniques, and body scans. All of these techniques allow you to reach a deep state of relaxation more quickly and effortlessly, so I encourage you to try them and see which ones work best for you!

Remember, even small actions can make a big difference when it comes to self-love and care, and establishing the best conditions for quick relaxation will do wonders!

Third Culture Kids

Even for the most adventurous, global souls among us, expat life takes on a whole new level of complexity once kids are involved. As parents, we feel ultimately responsible for the effect our choices may have on our little ones, and moving abroad certainly leaves a mark on them. For many families, living between cultures is a given - for instance, when parents come from different countries, or they've emigrated for good. For others, it's a choice - one that can lead to moments of doubt or guilt.

Children who have spent a significant amount of time outside their parents' culture(s) are called Third Culture Kids (TCKs). Exposed to diverse cultures and languages, they develop a unique worldview that incorporates elements of multiple cultures. TCKs often possess strong cross-cultural communication skills, understanding of different perspectives, a natural appreciation for diversity, and adaptability. Growing up in a bi- or multilingual environment may enhance cognitive abilities, problem-solving skills, creativity, and memory. Without a doubt, they're invaluable bridge builders in our global community and have the power to bring people together, mediate, and make our world a more inclusive and harmonious place.

To unlock their full potential and nurture their unique abilities, parents play a crucial role in guiding their Third Culture Kids, encouraging them to see the benefits of their diverse experiences even in challenging times - which they will also face along the way. For instance, many TCKs struggle with a sense of rootlessness, not knowing where to 'call home.' Grounding them in family traditions while maintaining connections to both parental backgrounds can provide a solid foundation for their identity.

In my experience, ensuring my TCKs visited my home country, Austria, regularly and spending quality time with my family and our long-standing friends turned out to be a game-changer. These visits not only allowed them to form a real connection to their Austrian roots, without actually living there; they also boosted their confidence, making it easier for them to interact with different people. I've always believed that giving our TCKs a solid ground to stand on helps them become open-minded global citizens. It's a balancing act to enable them to embrace their diverse backgrounds while feeling rooted and grounded wherever they go.

Another challenge experienced by many TCKs is forming lasting friendships amid frequent moves. As parents, we can help our children maintain friendships despite the geographical distance by helping them write letters, lending them our phones, or planning visits. On the other hand, fostering friendships with other TCKs in our current country of residence can give them a sense of familiarity, camaraderie, and an outlet to share their very unique experiences or struggles.

As a parent, it's important to sensitively respond to the needs of your Third Culture Kids and create a supportive environment for them. Actively listen to their concerns, validate their emotions, and establish routines that can provide some stability throughout their international lifestyle.

CREATING A STRONG FAMILY CULTURE ABROAD

I've always liked to think that families living abroad have the possibility to create a particularly strong bond; their unique identity and experience can bring family members closer together and foster a strong sense of belonging to the family unit. I've tried my best to create a strong family culture abroad. Here are a few things that have helped me achieve that while validating and normalizing their experience as TCKs:

MULTICULTURAL BEDTIME STORIES

Did your parents tell you stories when you were a kid that you still fondly remember? My husband and I have that in common. I can still vividly remember the stories my parents told me when I was little. Stories connect and bring people together.

After our last move, I invented a multicultural story of an Austrian garbage man (my boys were obsessed with garbage trucks when they were little!) who moved to the Basque Country and needed to navigate life and work in this new environment. These stories not only entertained my kids, they also sparked curiosity about cultural differences and helped them normalize and validate their own experiences.

THEME NIGHTS

Family dinners are important; and when you live abroad, why not spice things up a bit? Try incorporating different themes, like one evening dedicated to your country of heritage, one from your spouse's (if different), and one from the country you're currently living in. Involve your kids in meal preparation - they can always contribute somehow, no matter their age. Play national music, decorate the table accordingly, and, of course, share lots of stories!

FAMILY PLAYLISTS

Music was my world growing up, and sharing favorite songs with others made me feel connected. Does it do the same for your family? Create a playlist where each family member chooses and adds songs, in different languages and from the various countries you've lived in. It'll sweeten up those car rides and effectively anchor memories that often come to life again through music. Remember to keep an open mind. Even if you can't stand your teenager's taste in music, make an effort to find something you like about it, whether it's the beat, the voice, or the guitar riff. After all, it's about growing closer and inviting everyone to contribute to your family culture!

ADOPTING A NEW PERSPECTIVE

Living abroad blurs the standards you held for yourself and your family back home - and I love that! What you 'had to' do, wear, and live like back home may not be the same in your new country. It's an amazing opportunity to let go of old images and beliefs, which is especially important in parenting. Parents knowingly or unknowingly tend to seek validation through their children's behavior and accomplishments. Abroad, you can more easily stop comparing your kids to their peers and create space for their authentic selves to unfold. Step back and curiously figure out who you and your kids really are, away from everything. You might be surprised! Discovering and accepting your child's unique spirit is the greatest gift you can give them. Plus, it will undoubtedly make you feel much more connected to each other.

In closing, I hope these ideas inspire you to create a unique, cross-cultural family culture that will provide your Third Culture Kids with a strong sense of belonging, rootedness, continuity, and safety! Your family's journey is unique and building a strong bond can help you better face challenges together and celebrate the good times, wherever you are in the world.

Uncertainty

Being an expat and dealing with uncertainty kind of goes hand in hand. As global nomads, we face uncertainty on multiple fronts.

Take, for instance, what I call the 'Expat Limbo': the constant back-and-forth most serial expats experience when another relocation shows up on the horizon. Will we move? When? And where to?

Then there's the big unknown: "What will life be like in the new country?", "Will I be happy there?", and "What about my family?"

For self-initiated expats, the dilemma of "Should I stay or should I go?" can become a haunting question, keeping them up at night and causing them headaches.

On the other hand, long-term expats may find themselves wondering, "Will I ever move back home?" and "Where will I eventually call home?"

Everyone responds to uncertainty differently. According to Tony Robbins' *6 Human Needs*, we all have a need for both certainty (safety, security, predictability) and uncertainty (variety, adventure, unpredictability). However, the extent to which your emotional well-being relies on certainty can vary. If you're someone who values stability and always having a clear plan, the expat lifestyle might be a bit more challenging for you.

When faced with uncertainty, people typically react in one of two ways: some try to distract themselves, while others get stuck in rumination, worry, and stress. Clearly, neither of these is a good coping mechanism.

Instead, let's take a different approach. Let's admit to ourselves that, yes, not knowing what the future holds, where we'll live, and how our lives will turn out is really hard. These dilemmas aren't unique to you, and after talking to countless Expat Women, I can assure you that you're not alone.

But here's the key: it's not actually about the uncertainty we face, but about how we handle it. Let me show you by diving deeper into those typical uncertainty-related questions we often ask ourselves. Take, for instance: "What if I won't be happy in my next host country?" The underlying fear here is that you may not know how to make the best of the experience and how to find happiness in this new place. A subtle but significant difference.

If you're asking yourself: "Should I stay here or move back home?", the real struggle is often not so much the decision itself, but the fear of not being able to cope with the consequences, whatever they may be.

Sound familiar? If it does, you've just changed the game. You've shifted from an external problem, i.e. about a country, to an internal one, about yourself. The first may be hard to change, but the latter is entirely within your circle of influence. In essence, beneath all the uncertainty lies the fear that *you* won't be able to handle the consequences, make the best of it, and thrive under your given circumstances. It's less about the uncertainty itself and more about trusting yourself to navigate challenges.

Building up this self-trust is your superpower for handling uncertainty! How? By showing yourself that you are resilient, step by step. Think of all the times you managed to endure and overcome a struggle in your life. You did it then, and you can do it again.

Find a 'safe area' in your life to practice resilience – it could be resisting your urge to snack in between meals, doing one more push-up when you think you absolutely can't, taking the stairs instead of the elevator, or waking up 15 minutes earlier than usual. All of these things might seem insignificant, but they're a testament to your inner strength and resilience, and will reassure you of them.

Also, don't forget to show up as the CEO of your life, as discussed in Chapter B - Becoming Your Own Biggest Ally. When those worries start to get loud, your CEO can choose not to get caught up in them, and to challenge them with more constructive or optimistic voices. To foster self-trust, it's crucial for your mind to be a safe place to inhabit. So always, always be kind to yourself, and forgive yourself when you mess up. We all do, and it's what makes us human.

Finally, I encourage you to wholeheartedly commit to giving your best in life, regardless of circumstances. Make a vow to yourself that you will always do whatever you can and whatever it takes, so that when you look back you can feel good about yourself. Also, trust that you did the best you could at that moment, even if the result wasn't what you hoped for. This will not only strengthen your self-trust muscles but also free yourself from having regrets after taking a decision.

So, when uncertainty knocks on your door, acknowledge its presence and complexity. But focus on your ability to make the best of any situation and to influence the outcome. It's not about eliminating uncertainty; it's about thriving despite it!

Vision

Many expats will move abroad more than once and become *pros* at starting over in a new place. With such an international lifestyle, it's no surprise that much of your time and energy will go into planning, packing, and settling in. And once that's done, your next relocation might already be on the horizon.

It's not easy to cultivate a long-term vision when you're so caught up in the short and mid-term hassles of a relocation. And yet, let me show you why it's so important that you do.

I'm sure you're familiar with Maslow's pyramid of the hierarchy of needs, which below I've adapted to Expat Life. Here's what it entails, from bottom to top:

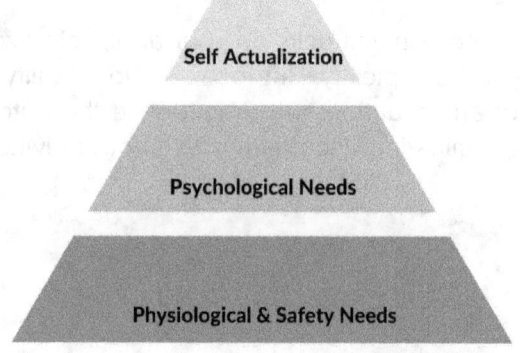

PHYSIOLOGICAL AND SAFETY NEEDS

For expats, this involves determining where you'll move, where you'll live, your work, your children's school, and familiarizing yourself with local surroundings, culture, lifestyle, and language.

PSYCHOLOGICAL NEEDS

These include making new friends, creating a support system, finding a sense of belonging, feeling seen, heard, validated and respected.

SELF-ACTUALIZATION

This is about finding meaning and a sense of purpose in life, growing as a person, expressing your authentic self, and making a valuable contribution and impact.

Now, what I've noticed throughout years of working with Expat Women is that they're often busy tackling the demands of the lower pyramid at the cost of developing the top part.

If you're someone who moves regularly, it can be tempting to think of your life in terms of assignments: 2 years here, 3 years there, 4 years somewhere else. But this can put you at risk of waking up one day, wondering what it is you've actually done, and what you should do next?

Having witnessed several existential crises as a result of a globally mobile lifestyle, I'd like to remind you of this: Your different assignments and destinations should be different chapters of the same book. It's essential to develop a long-term vision and create a life story that's meaningful, purposeful, and that guides you along your international journey, no matter where it takes you.

The way you'll live out your vision may look different, depending on the circumstances you encounter in each place. But nevertheless, whatever you do should be like another puzzle piece of the big picture you want to create. And if at any point in your expat life you feel lost, or lack meaning and joy in what you do: focus on the big picture you want to create. Many of the problems you encounter are actually just symptoms of lacking a bigger vision and a higher purpose.

Maslow suggested that self-actualization is the pinnacle of human needs, and it's usually achieved after fulfilling the more foundational ones. For global women fortunate enough to meet those, it's therefore not just an opportunity but a privilege and responsibility to pursue true and lasting self-actualization; this goes way beyond personal satisfaction and involves contributing to others' well-being, committing to a greater cause and creating a positive ripple effect.

BRINGING YOUR VISION TO LIFE

The vehicle to reach self-actualization, despite several relocations and changing circumstances, is to have a compelling vision of the future you want to create for yourself. It will serve as a roadmap, guiding you in making decisions, setting goals, and taking actions that align with your values and aspirations.

To help you define your own vision, I invite you to reflect on the following questions:

- What's always true about me, no matter where I am and what I do?

- What skills and gifts of mine light me up and bring joy to others?

- When I look back at who I've been and what I've done in my life at old age, what do I want to see?

- How would I like to be remembered when I'm gone?

- What are some essential, non-negotiable things I absolutely want to achieve, experience or create in this lifetime?
- Who are my biggest role-models and why?
- What positive impact do I want to make - in my family, community, workplace, and in the world?

I recommend writing down the answers to these questions and to verbally process them with someone. Thoughts can be fleeting, but there's so much power in writing them down or speaking them out. Also, it will give you the chance to look back on your notes in the future and remember your previous insights.

Though the essence and core of your big vision will probably stay the same, you might alter and add to it. That's okay, your vision is supposed to be alive, to grow with you and take on even more detailed forms.

The last question, "What positive impact do I want to make?", is particularly important and often overlooked. Reason being that we are much more likely to meet (and fight for) goals that are 'bigger than ourselves'. If you can clearly see how pursuing your long-term vision will improve not only your own quality of life but also that of your loved ones, your community, or humanity as a whole... you have a powerful motivator and driving force to draw energy and resources from!

Furthermore, you'll be able to more easily overcome self-doubt that would otherwise hold you back – after all, this isn't just about you but about the positive impact you're making.

As I like to say: "A woman with a vision is a woman on a mission and SHE is unstoppable!" When you clearly know which way you're headed, you'll figure everything else out.

Having a vision will give you a sense of meaning, purpose and direction. But if you don't act on it, you won't be able to bring it to life. So as a next step, break your vision down into achievable goals and create an action plan. The great thing about your life's bigger vision is that there's (hopefully!) a lot of room and time for it to unfold. There's no need to rush things. Rather than the destination, your journey is the actual goal and reward.

Developing a bigger vision for your life is a big endeavor. You can access more valuable exercises to achieve this at www.camillaquintana.com/book

Winning Mindsets

The way we think and the attitude we carry is directly related to the kind of life we'll lead. My own core lesson in life has been that it's a constant dance between seeing the glass half full and seeing it half empty. No matter what we're going through at any given moment, both perspectives are always available to us.

As a matter of fact, if other people could walk in your shoes, you'd find that some of them would focus on what you lack while others would focus on what you've got. There's no objective answer to your subjective realities and perceptions. The glass is neither really full or empty. It's what we make it out to be. And we can choose to either see the opportunities, the ways out, the things to be grateful for... or to focus on what's not going well and what we're missing.

Our challenge is to train ourselves to see the glass half full more and more often. This requires strength, a lot of awareness and sometimes a leap of faith. But when you do: you will stand in your power, proactively shaping and creating the best conditions for you to thrive, no matter what and no matter where.

I like to think of our mindset, the state of mind we cultivate, as the container for our thoughts. The traits of this container sort of sets the scene and influences what kind of thoughts come more easily to us than others.

Did you know that behind every pattern, habit, and repeated action or thought is a neural pathway? These pathways enable communication between our cells. The more we repeat a specific behavior or thought, the stronger these neural connections become. In some cases, an action may even become automatic, like the routine act of brushing your teeth or driving a car.

The brain's ability to create and strengthen these neural connections is called Neuroplasticity. It refers to the process through which the brain rewires itself in response to changes in the environment or behavior. This proven capacity of our brain to change and adapt, regardless of age, is precisely what empowers us to modify our thoughts and habits. I believe that by cultivating a powerful and constructive mindset, we create the kind of container in which empowering thoughts will be able to flourish!

I like to use the symbol of the container, because we'll all go through phases in which positive thoughts come more easily to us, and others in which they won't. Despite fostering an empowering mindset, it's only natural for your thoughts to fluctuate. Thanks to the container, however, they won't be spiraling down in free fall but merely drop to its bottom. This will make it easier for you to pick yourself up again when you've experienced hardship or inner turmoil.

Over the years, I've developed and adopted 3 mindset hacks that have positively influenced my thoughts and rewired my brain for constructive thinking. I'm sure they'll be as valuable to you as they have been for me and my clients:

Winning Mindset No. 1:
THE COUNTER-THOUGHT

Several years ago, I was swimming all by myself in the pool of my neighborhood. It was just at the time when we were preparing our move away from my hometown, Vienna to Bilbao, where my husband was relocated to for work.

As I did my lengths, I had time to contemplate the effect our upcoming move would have on us: Taking my two small sons out of the kindergarten they loved going to, and enrolling them in a different country in two separate institutions (due to their age); moving out of the home we'd been so happy in, into a small, temporary apartment; and most importantly, leaving behind our family and friends, to whom we had such close bonds that I dreaded losing...

These thoughts weighed heavily on me, so in an attempt to distract myself, I started playing a little game.

At first it was just a fun thing to do but soon I noticed how this subtle mind hack changed everything in my life: the way I interpreted things, the way I responded to things and how quickly I could get back on track after the 'disturbances' we all face in life.

Here's what I did: Everytime I had an unpleasant, fearful thought or made some kind of value judgment, I challenged myself to think one opposite or one positive thought about the situation.

STEP 1: Become aware of your fearful thoughts or the snap judgements you make. From the "What ifs" to the "I don't like this" or "It shouldn't be this way". You'll be surprised to see how often your mind engages in this kind of thinking automatically, without even noticing it.

STEP 2: Counter your negative thoughts with one opposite or positive perspective. Ideally, it's an honest one. But if you can't come up with anything sincere, just think something – anything – with an opposite meaning and contemplate how that could hold some truth as well.

In my case, I shifted from the fearful thought of: "What if moving abroad will make me lose my close friendships back home?" to the empowering Counter-Thought: "What if moving away will actually bring me even closer to my loved ones? How could this be true?" I can't begin to tell you how many ideas started pouring in once I was able to look at the situation from a different perspective. Thanks to counter-thinking I was able to successfully nurture my most important bonds over the distance.

While the original thought is heavy, limiting, painful, the counter-thought - though confusing at first - prompts you to think outside the box: what could be a different take on this? How could I make the opposite happen? What other answers, explanations or solutions might there be that I haven't thought about before?

Remember, nothing has meaning unless we give it to it. So let's be open for alternative interpretations and outcomes. Of course, you don't have to force yourself to see the good in something you consider bad, as that would only create resistance and be counterproductive. This exercise trains your mind to be able to access different kinds of thoughts and realities, and explore how or whether they, too, could be true.

As you rewire your brain and adopt new ways of thinking, you'll become more and more resourceful. I encourage you to turn counter-thinking into a mindset, forming the container around your fears, judgements and evaluations. This way you'll ensure that you won't be able to allow an unpleasant or unintentional thought to run wild inside your mind, without at the very least contrasting it with a more empowering one!

Winning Mindset No. 2:
REACH FOR THE NEXT, BETTER-FEELING THOUGHT

This is something I read in an Abraham Hicks book and found so helpful. When you're having an unpleasant or fearful thought, ask yourself: "What is the next better-feeling thought I can think of?" It should be something you can believe and have no resistance to, so that you can exchange your first thought with a 'lesser evil'.

This is not to be confused with affirmations or with positive thinking per se. It's also not the same as the Counter-Thought exercise which is really more about learning to see things differently. This exercise is about noticing your current thoughts, and finding ways to upgrade them, in a way that it still feels true and believable to you.

Example:

- Thought: I put on so much weight over the holidays.
- Next, better-feeling thought (still believable and honoring your discontent): I put on belly-weight. But my legs are fine.

Get into the habit of chasing better-feeling thoughts and turn this into a mindset, so that the quality of your thinking will continue to improve. Especially if you're struggling with a vocal inner critic or excessive worry, this exercise will help you to look at yourself and your life in a more nuanced, compassionate and constructive way!

Winning Mindset No. 3:
I'M LIVING THE DREAM!

When I first came up with this mindset hack, I called it: This is the best time of my life!

As a disclaimer: I do not recommend this to people who are currently or chronically feeling depressed (in that case, please refer to Mindset No. 2).

Let me tell you how I came up with the idea of 'living the dream'.

One night (I was home alone and therefore had Couch Commando) I decided to watch a light-hearted chick flick. In the opening scene, you saw a gorgeous young woman, rolling out of bed and looking fabulous. She got dressed for work (very stylishly, of course), and then walked to her office in high heels, coffee in hand, smiling confidently as her hair bounced in the wind. She went into her office building where everyone greeted her warmly, and proceeded to give a killer presentation to a group of clients, landing the much anticipated contract for her company. Soon after, she met her lovely fiancé for lunch and....

... I caught myself thinking: "Wow, she's living the dream!"

"Huh. Interesting", another voice in my head said. "So she is *acting* like she's living the dream. This actress is convincing me that this is what living the dream looks like, and as a viewer, I'm perceiving that."

Of course, later on you find out that she's not perfect, she loses her job, her fiancé and has to start over from scratch. But the idea stuck with me:

What happens when I believe and act like 'I'm living the dream'? Or that 'this is the best time of my life'? How would I show up if this were the case? How would I act? What opportunities would I see and take advantage of?

I love experimenting with myself and so I decided to give it a try. Every time I got in the car or went for a walk, I would tell myself that I was living the dream. I even came up with little rhymes and songs, repeating them over and over for my subconsciousness. And then I'd look for reasons why this could actually really be the case.

In the times I struggled to come up with reasons, I'd think: "If looking back, this would turn out to be the best time of my life: What would I appreciate more about it? What would I take more advantage of?"

If you're currently in a good place, this mindset hack is a great way to appreciate and feel grateful for everything you've got! To bask in your joy, dwell in your bliss, and allow yourself to feel happy about life.

And if you're currently in a low state of mind, facing adversity, think about the people who are going through something even worse and would give a lot to trade places. Or could it be that life isn't so grim after all? Maybe there are beautiful things about your life you've forgotten to acknowledge, because you were so focused on what's missing, or what's not working well.

How could you be living the dream right now?

Remember, your mindset sets the stage for the kind of life you'll lead, and with these intentional shifts, you can create a more empowering narrative!

X
XXX Your Life Abroad

There's a powerful quote by Marianne Williamson that resonates deeply: *"Our deepest fear is not that we are inadequate. Our deepest fear is that we are powerful beyond measure. It is our light, not our darkness that most frightens us. We ask ourselves, 'Who am I to be brilliant, gorgeous, talented, fabulous?'"*

Throughout history, women have been conditioned to prioritize others' needs, be humble, and settle for what they had. Society often discouraged them from pursuing ambitious goals, labeling those as selfish or unattainable. Even today, being bold, assertive, and confident can expose women to criticism or worse.

But here's a radical thought: What if everything you desire and dream about isn't audacious at all but merely a fraction of what you're destined to experience? What if those goals you thought were 'too much to ask for' are actually too small, and you are meant for even more? I got this idea from self-made billionaire Grant Cardone, and the minute I read about it in his book, *The 10X Rule*, I was convinced and inspired.

Here's the thing: Setting big goals is incredibly motivating. It pushes you to think outside the box, find new and innovative approaches, and consequently, become much more efficient. Plus, even if you fall short of accomplishing the big goal, you'll still likely make more progress overall than you would have if you had chased a smaller, less exciting one.

When you settle for uninspiring, safe goals that don't demand pushing your limits, you actually risk achieving the opposite effect. The resulting underwhelm, even if subtle, can lead to procrastination, self-doubt, or analysis paralysis. As a consequence, your motivation, drive, and self-trust may fade, making it increasingly difficult to see your project through. Also, falling short of a small goal feels more disheartening than not quite reaching a big one. So, embrace the audacity of your dreams, set larger goals, and believe in your ability and worthiness to reach them!

At this point, you might be thinking: "All this talk about big goals sounds kind of stressful and overly ambitious!" And I get it. In self-help literature there's certainly a focus on reducing stress, which evidently is so unhealthy for our minds and bodies. Words like 'ambition' and 'accomplishments' quickly get a negative connotation, after all, we're reminded that we're human beings, not 'human doings'.

Our innate worth isn't tied to our actions or results. We all matter as we are, and are unique in our own special way. Spreading this message is vital for mental health, diversity, and social equity. It's also crucial in parenting, so that we can teach our kids that we love them just the way they are, thus encouraging them to love, and respect themselves regardless of their achievements.

And yet, there's also another side to the story.

THE RISK OF BEING UNDERCHALLENGED

Having specialized in the syndrome of Boreout in Expat Wives, I can tell you that the chronic mental underload, lack of fulfillment and meaning they experience are extremely painful. I don't want you to look back one day, and not feel proud of who you've become and of what you've done. Because this, too, is a hazard for your mental health, your self-esteem, your relationships, and your overall well-being in life.

We need to actively work on making the best of our life abroad - and anywhere! This is where your inspiring goals and your ambition to accomplish them come into play:

In Chapter C and Chapter V, we talked about why you need to have a long-term vision, and set goals to make it a reality. A life without ambitious and meaningful goals is the gateway to spiraling thoughts, worry, anxiety, unhappiness, boredom, and even Boreout. There's also solid scientific evidence supporting the importance of accomplishments. For instance, it's considered one of the five key elements for human well-being according to the field of Positive Psychology.

So maybe it's not about rejecting having ambition and striving for accomplishments, but rather reframing what they mean and what value they can bring to our lives? Maybe it's not about being on either side but finding the fine line between healthy and unhealthy ambition and drive?

The key to a healthy approach is found in the relationship with yourself. Never push yourself out of a sense of unworthiness. Instead, embrace your ambitions as a reflection of your intrinsic worth and potential. If you decide to reach the next iteration of your life, do it because you know you are meant to shine and make a difference.

So let me ask you this:

- Do you think there's more to life than what you're currently experiencing?

- Do you feel like you're not yet tapping into your full potential?

- Would you like to XXX your life abroad?

If your answers are "Yes!", I invite you to take the following

7 STEPS TO XXX YOUR LIFE ABROAD

1. Visualize something big you'd really like to achieve or see happen in your life, even though it may seem scary, unrealistic or 'out there'.

2. Write your big goal down, and be specific.

3. Give yourself a short deadline: it should be doable, but still tight. This will allow you to start with a bang, gain momentum, create some urgency around your goal and proactively think about how you could finish it in the most efficient way possible.

4. Mark your calendar: set aside uninterrupted time during which you'll work on your goal. If you can't do it alone, schedule meetings with the other involved parties beforehand.

5. Exploit resources: Could you carve out some more time to work on your big goal? Could you improve the quality of your sleep, in order to be more productive and fresh throughout the day? What will you need to delegate or say no to? Who could help you? Who could you collaborate with?

6. Write down your progress in a journal: every night, before going to bed, take notes of what you've done to achieve your big goal, what's gone well and what you want to improve next time.

7. Plan out your next day: Have an agenda of things you will do tomorrow, so that you can start your day with intention.

BONUS STEP: SELF-CARE & SURRENDERING

Things can come up unexpectedly and you might need to press pause on your ambitious endeavor. That's normal, so don't resist it - plan for it and work with it.

Trust me, I'd know: When I was writing this book, I applied this exact strategy. My initial plan was to finish writing the book in one month's time. By the time my deadline came around, the manuscript was about 90% finished. But then, due to some personal and family issues, I completely fell off track. It took months to get back into writing and editing, and I took it slow. This experience taught me the following:

1. The above strategy is extremely powerful, after all I got extremely close to finishing writing a book in only 30 days!

2. Things can come up and distract us from our goals. If we can't change it, we must accept it, have lots of self-compassion, patience and trust in ourselves to carry on.

3. Once you fall off track and lose momentum, it's really hard to pick up the pace again. It might help to take some time off, and then re-apply the XXX strategy.

Self-Care should become part of your lifestyle, and nourishing yourself a priority. Sometimes this will indeed look like slowing down and resting. Other times this means putting your phone away, shutting the door and ambitiously working on making your wildest dreams come true!

Yearning For Home

There's a widespread belief floating around on social media and within the coaching industry, suggesting that if you only try hard enough, you can be happy wherever you live.

I respectfully disagree. Just as a flower requires good soil to thrive, so do you. The type of soil or environment you need depends on your unique values, goals, and needs.

For example, if you value your family and childhood friends above all else, putting relationships first, living abroad could be difficult. Family holds an irreplaceable place in our lives, which becomes especially apparent when dealing with aging parents or receiving bad news from home. Additionally, forming deep connections takes time, and in expat circles, people often come and go, leaving a void.

Or let's consider another scenario: Suppose you're driven to build a successful career and achieve financial independence. Even if you've established a wonderful circle of friends abroad, and live in a beautiful home in a great location... if you're unable to work, develop your career, or earn an attractive salary in that country, you ultimately won't be satisfied.

Again for others, it might be of utmost importance to live and raise their children in a certain environment that aligns with their values, perhaps shaped by their religion.

Just as every person prioritizes certain aspects of life over others, each country also represents and fosters particular values and opportunities more than others. In that sense, some places will be very fertile ground for you. Others can become that with the right fertilizer. Again others may simply make it very difficult for you to flourish.

As an Expat Coach, I help my clients to learn how to fertilize the soil they live on intensively. But, not at all costs. My focus on fostering Radical Self-Love and Awareness and on pursuing your unique long-term vision brings great clarity to your life. It will help you determine what helps you flourish and what doesn't.

LISTEN TO YOUR INNER KNOWING

If you've had a lingering feeling that you've somehow exhausted the opportunities and possibilities in your host country and that there aren't enough reasons or people for you to stay there, it's important to pay attention. It could be a phase of Expat Fatigue (see chapter E - Expat Fatigue). But if the feeling continues, it might be time for a change.

Sometimes this can feel like a failure on your end: Could you be giving up too quickly? Should you be able to hang in there and stick it out? What will others think of your decision to move away? Other times, especially when other family members are involved, it can make you feel selfish and wrong for wanting to move away: Is this really the best decision for everyone? Is one person's unhappiness reason enough to move the whole family to another country? Or vice versa, is one person's happiness or success reason enough for the whole family to stay?

Relationships can suffer greatly when one partner wants to move away and the other doesn't. A change of scenery can sometimes help conflicted couples to experience a much needed reset. A fresh start offers the possibility to establish new habits and dynamics, which can be very healthy for your romantic life.

If you feel conflicted about your desire to move away, that's only natural: A relocation is a big life transition. There's usually some uncertainty about what's on the other side, what you can expect - and whether those expectations will be met. Let the trust in yourself, in your intuition and in a higher power be what guides you through this confusing phase:

First of all, recognize, acknowledge, and honor that 'icky feeling' that signals when things in your current location aren't working for you anymore, or when you simply miss home (or any place that feels like it to you) too much.

We often try to ignore or distract ourselves from that icky feeling. However, I've come to view it as a blessing! If I hadn't paid attention to and addressed that feeling, my life would be completely different now, and by that I mean worse. I would have remained in situations that weren't right for me and wasted my energy on things that didn't bring me joy, instead of making a change. These days, I approach that icky feeling with curiosity whenever it arises within me. I see it as my ally, guiding me toward positive change and improving the quality of my life.

So, make peace with that inner voice that whispers it's time to leave. It's not a sign of weakness or selfishness, but simply your inner truth. Allow yourself to sit with it and get to know it. Talk or journal about your feelings and thoughts. Take some time to better understand what exactly you're dissatisfied with and what you need to feel better. Also, connect with your long-term vision and the vision you hold for your family and children. This might just be the compelling reason and motivation you need to make a change.

But above all, trust. Trust in your inner truth and in your decision. Trust in yourself to be able to make the best of your choice and of its consequences. You deserve to:

- flourish
- have people who love and care for you nearby
- have access to fulfilling work and professional opportunities
- live safely and free from excessive worry
- unfold your potential
- make yourself a priority
- pursue your calling, purpose, and heart projects
- make a difference
- be happy

YOU'RE HERE TO BLOOM.

So, it's okay to be picky with the soil you grow on. Make an effort to nurture, manure, water and weed it. But if nothing works: go and bloom elsewhere.

Z
Zest For Global Living

Those of us who have lived abroad know that a part of our heart will always remain there. We will be forever marked by the memories we've made, the places we've seen, the people we've befriended, the flavors we've tasted, the music we've danced to, the customs we've adopted, the differences we've come to love, and the profound experience of seeing ourselves through a different lens. All of that is of immeasurable value and will enrich your life forever.

As global women, we have the privilege of knowing different views, perspectives, ways, possibilities, and realities - and leveraging them in addition to the ones we already knew. With that privilege comes responsibility. It's global citizens like us who can bring the world closer together, connect people of different backgrounds, see beyond borders, races, or religions, and foster intercultural understanding. By using our knowledge and resources for good, we'll inspire others to embrace the wonderful diversity of our Planet Earth.

I've been thinking about just how much my time abroad has shaped me and what it means for people to cultivate a zest for global living. Here's what I came up with:

YOU EMBRACE DIFFERENT CULTURES

You're open to new experiences abroad and appreciate the differences. You take the time to explore your new surroundings, try the local cuisine, and learn about the customs and traditions of the local people. Some of the local dishes will go into your cooking repertoire, songs into your playlists, and celebrations into your calendar and family life. You're excited about fully immersing yourself in a different country and curious about what you'll discover.

YOU LEARN FOREIGN LANGUAGES

Being able to communicate with locals, to better understand cultural premises and origins, and to radically increase your opportunities abroad motivates you. As a global citizen, you probably even feel called to pick up more than one other language. You enjoy watching movies in their original language, reading local newspapers, writing down and memorizing new words and expressions, and practicing with native speakers whenever you get a chance. If you have an accent, see it as your trademark - it shows how far you've come, how much you've experienced, and can even serve as an ice-breaker.

YOU CONNECT DEEPLY WITH DIFFERENT PEOPLE

You have a natural interest in and curiosity about different people. The more countries, cultures, and people you know, the easier it becomes to start conversations - and interesting ones at that. Equipped with cultural sensitivity, empathy, and understanding, you're in a position to quickly create meaningful connections, and have done so many times. You enjoy bringing people together and introducing them to like-minded others. When you notice someone in need of help, you step in: after all, having experienced being a foreigner, you know how important it is to receive support, kindness, and care.

YOU EMBRACE YOURSELF

Life abroad has deepened your connection with yourself and your inner happy place. It has transformed you into your own biggest ally, constantly advocating for your well-being, success, fulfillment, and happiness. Navigating outside your comfort zone, experiencing loneliness, inadequacy, and feeling lost and confused along your journey has served to heighten your awareness of your needs and desires at any given moment.

You understand that your sense of identity is a fluid concept, valuable only if it brings out the best in you, allows you to unfold your potential, and live authentically and happily. The experience of moving abroad has prompted you to reinvent yourself, and you're not afraid to do it again if necessary. You are the one who defines who you want to be, and you genuinely embrace the person you are becoming.

YOU APPROACH THE WORLD WITH AN OPEN MIND AND CURIOSITY

You recognize the diverse ways of doing, thinking, and perceiving, understanding that none is inherently better or worse than the others. Different realities coexist, and there is no absolute truth. Cultural conditioning is real, and it influences all of us. Living abroad has honed your ability to pick up on subtle nuances and has sharpened your problem-solving skills. When seeking answers and solutions, you go the extra mile. Instead of making unfounded assumptions, you prefer to ask insightful questions. You don't stay on the surface but aim to get to the bottom of things.

YOU EMBRACE DIVERSITY

Simple explanations, generalizations, and stereotypes don't resonate with you. You don't put people into a box (cultural or otherwise) because you know that it always fails to truly grasp the complexity of an individual. Being exposed to different people and cultures has made you appreciate and celebrate differences rather than viewing them as barriers. The experience of being the foreigner and the odd one out allowed you to empathize with minority groups and be more sensitive to their struggles. You know that everyone has their place and that we're all interconnected. We all have many different facets to be discovered, and you don't shy away from exploring yours.

Ultimately, cultivating a zest for Global Living is an ongoing journey. It's vital for making the most out of your life abroad and ensuring that your vibrant experiences will keep adding value, no matter where you find yourself!

FINAL WORDS

Wow, can you believe it? We've reached the end of this book! I want to take a moment to express my heartfelt gratitude for sharing this adventure with me.

Over the years, I've had the privilege of connecting with an incredible community of Expat Women, who've inspired the content within these pages.

Living abroad is a journey unlike any other, and it will shape you in ways you never imagined. While this book has served as a compass, the real journey begins when you put these pages down. So, rather than a farewell, let's see it as the beginning of your next chapter!

You are the author of your story, and every twist and turn is an opportunity to discover something new about yourself. Embrace each moment as an invitation to take action and apply everything you've learned here into your life.

For ongoing support, keep this book close, like a trusted friend you can turn to whenever you need reassurance or a fresh perspective. With its independent chapters, you can easily dive in and out, and find solace and inspiration whenever you need it.

Also, don't forget to download the complimentary resources available at www.camillaquintana.com/book to enhance your journey even further!

Remember, I'm here for you whenever you need a listening ear or a guiding hand along your expat journey. Whether you have questions, need advice and accountability, or simply want to share your experiences, I'm just a message away.

With love,

Camilla

www.ingramcontent.com/pod-product-compliance
Lightning Source LLC
Chambersburg PA
CBHW052151110526
44591CB00012B/1940